MW00529086

GOSPEL STUDIES SERIES

Your Study of

The Book of

Revelation

Made Easier

Second Edition

GOSPEL STUDIES SERIES

Your Study of

The Book of

Revelation

Made Easier

Second Edition

David J. Ridges

Springville, Utah

ISBN 13: 978-1-59955-418-1

Published by CFI, an imprint of Cedar Fort, Inc.
2373 W. 700 S., Springville, UT, 84663
Distributed by Cedar Fort, Inc., www.cedarfort.com

LIBRARY OF CONGRESS CATALOGING-IN-PUBLICATION DATA
Ridges, David J.
  The book of Revelation made easier / David J. Ridges.
    p. cm.
  ISBN 978-1-59955-418-1
  1. Bible. N.T. Revelation--Criticism, interpretation, etc. I. Title.

  BS2825.52.R54 2010
  228'.077--dc22
                              2010027468

Cover design by Nicole Williams
Cover design © 2010 by Lyle Mortimer
Edited by Heather Holm

Printed in the United States of America

10 9 8 7 6 5 4 3 2

Printed on acid-free paper

Books
by David J. Ridges

The Gospel Studies Series:

- *Isaiah Made Easier, Second Edition*
- *The New Testament Made Easier, Part 1 (Second Edition)*
- *The New Testament Made Easier, Part 2 (Second Edition)*
- *Your Study of The Book of Mormon Made Easier, Part 1*
- *Your Study of The Book of Mormon Made Easier, Part 2*
- *Your Study of The Book of Mormon Made Easier, Part 3*
- *Your Study of The Doctrine and Covenants Made Easier, Part 1*
- *Your Study of The Doctrine and Covenants Made Easier, Part 2*
- *Your Study of The Doctrine and Covenants Made Easier, Part 3*
- *The Old Testament Made Easier—Part 1*
- *The Old Testament Made Easier—Selections from the Old Testament, Part 2*
- *The Old Testament Made Easier—Selections from the Old Testament, Part 3*
- *Your Study of the Pearl of Great Price Made Easier*
- *Your Study of Jeremiah Made Easier*
- *Your Study of The Book of Revelation Made Easier, Second Edition*

Additional titles by David J. Ridges:

- *Our Savior, Jesus Christ: His Life and Mission to Cleanse and Heal*
- *Mormon Beliefs and Doctrines Made Easier*
- *The Proclamation on the Family: The Word of the Lord on More Than 30 Current Issues*
- *65 Signs of the Times and the Second Coming*
- *Doctrinal Details of the Plan of Salvation: From Premortality to Exaltation*

These titles will soon be available through
Cedar Fort as e-books and on CD.

THE GOSPEL STUDIES SERIES

Welcome to this volume of the Gospel Studies Series, which will take you through every verse of the book of Revelation, with brief notes and commentary within and between verses. It is designed to keep you in the scripture while providing instruction and help along the way.

As with other study guides in the Gospel Studies Series dealing with LDS scriptures, this work is intended to be a user-friendly, introductory study of Revelation, as well as a refresher course for more advanced students of the scriptures. It is also designed and formatted to be a quick-reference resource that will enable readers to easily look up a particular verse or set of verses and gain additional understanding regarding them. The author hopes that readers will write in the margins of their own scriptures some of the notes given in this study guide in order to assist them as they read and study Revelation in the future.

—David J. Ridges

THE JST REFERENCES IN
STUDY GUIDES BY DAVID J. RIDGES

Note that some of the JST (The Joseph Smith Translation of the Bible) references I use in my study guides are not found in our LDS Bible in the footnotes or in the Joseph Smith Translation section in the reference section in the back. The reason for this, as explained to me while writing curriculum materials for the Church, is simply that there is not enough room to include all of the JST additions and changes to the King James Version of the Bible (the one we use in the English speaking part of the Church). As you can imagine, as was likewise explained to me, there were difficult decisions that had to be made by the Scriptures Committee of the Church as to which JST contributions were included and which were not.

The Joseph Smith Translation of the Bible in its entirety can generally be found in or ordered through LDS bookstores. It was originally published under the auspices of the Reorganized Church of Jesus Christ of Latter Day Saints in Independence, Missouri. The version of the JST I prefer to use is a parallel column version, *Joseph Smith's "New Translation" of the Bible*, published by Herald Publishing House, Independence, Missouri, in 1970. This parallel column version compares the King James Bible with the JST side by side and includes only the verses that have changes, additions, or deletions made by the Prophet Joseph Smith.

By the way, some members of the Church have wondered whether or not we can trust the JST since it was published by a breakaway faction from our Church. They worry that some changes from Joseph Smith's original manuscript might have been made to support doctrinal differences between us and the RLDS Church. This is not the case. Many years ago, Robert J. Matthews of the Brigham Young University Religion Department was given permission by leaders of the RLDS Church to go to their Independence, Missouri, headquarters and personally compare the original JST document word for word with their publication of the JST. Brother Matthews was thus able to verify that they had been meticulously true to the Prophet's original work.

CONTENTS

FOREWORD

This second edition of *The Book of Revelation Made Easier* includes over 12,000 additional words of explanation and clarification compared to the first edition found in *Your Study of the New Testament Made Easier, Part 2, Acts through Revelation,* second edition, published in 2007.

Many members of the Church have considerable difficulty understanding the book of Revelation in the New Testament. They hear a lot about the prophecies of the last days contained in it, but when they attempt to read and understand it for themselves, they get discouraged and often give up. This study guide is formatted and designed to remedy that problem. It makes your study of Revelation easier (not necessarily easy) and can give you virtually an instant, basic understanding of this vital and fascinating book of scripture.

Rather than discussing how to go about studying the revelation of John the Beloved, this study guide is designed to help you actually *do* it. You will find the guide to scriptural symbolism on page 3 most helpful, because biblical and cultural symbolism, commonly understood in New Testament times, can be a difficult stumbling block for us in our day. Brief notes within and between verses serve to help you understand, while keeping you right in the scripture itself, where the power of the word of God resides.

This manual is not intended to be the final word on the meaning and interpretation of Revelation. Rather, it is designed to help you see possible interpretations and major messages that can give you a feel for the greatness of this prophetic book. I am hopeful that you will then, with the help of the Spirit, see many other possibilities and messages to assist you in gaining exaltation.

David J. Ridges

THE REVELATION
OF ST JOHN THE DIVINE

The Prophet Joseph said, "The book of Revelation is one of the plainest books God ever caused to be written" (Smith, *Teachings of the Prophet Joseph Smith*, p. 290). This statement by the Prophet is a reminder that this marvelous book of scripture can be understood. In fact, we are greatly blessed to have much inspired help as we seek to read and understand it. Elder Bruce R. McConkie of the Quorum of the Twelve Apostles said the following:

> As a matter of fact, we are in a much better position to understand those portions of Revelation which we are expected to understand than we generally realize. Thanks be to the interpretive material found in sections 29, 77, 88, and others of the revelations in the Doctrine and Covenants; plus the revisions given in the Inspired Version of the Bible [*the Joseph Smith Translation of the Bible*]; plus the sermons of the Prophet; plus some clarifying explanations in the Book of Mormon and other latter-day scripture; plus our overall knowledge of the plan of salvation—thanks be to all of these things (to say nothing of a little conservative sense, wisdom and inspiration in their application), the fact is that we have a marvelously comprehensive and correct under-standing of this otherwise hidden book (McConkie, *Doctrinal New Testament Commentary*, 3:431).

One of our real advantages in studying and understanding the book of Revelation, as mentioned by Elder McConkie in the above quote, is that we have been taught the plan of salvation. The book of Revelation presents the plan of salvation as seen against the background of the last days, when evil and wickedness will finally come to an end as the Millennium is ushered in by the Second Coming of the Savior. Again, since we have been taught the plan of salvation, we are in a much better position to understand Revelation than others who are not familiar with the restored gospel.

The JST (the Joseph Smith Translation of the Bible) makes changes in over eighty verses of the book of Revelation and thus becomes one of our most valuable keys for understanding John's writings in this book of the New Testament.

Still, for most members of the Church, Revelation is somewhat intimidating when it comes to reading it and trying to understand it. With that in mind, this study guide has been written in a way that keeps you in the scriptures themselves, where the real power is, while providing brief, to-the-point notes within and between the verses. The notes are somewhat conversational and are designed to provide instant understanding of John's inspired writings on a basic level. As is always the case, the Holy Ghost can give additional understanding and application. It is hoped that you will mark your own scriptures and make many notes in the margins so that this study guide will continue to aid you throughout your life in your study of Revelation.

General Background

The Apostle John wrote the book of Revelation in about AD 95. He was the brother of James and one of the original Twelve called by Jesus. He came to be known as John the Beloved because of the special fondness Jesus felt for him (John 13:23). He was in the presidency of the early Church with Peter and James after the Savior's ascension into heaven. He is the author of the Gospel of John, First John, Second John, Third John, and the book of Revelation. He is still alive, having been given the special privilege of being allowed to live on the earth as a translated being until the Savior's Second Coming. (See John 21:21–23; D&C 7.) Little more is recorded of his life except for the brief mention in Revelation of his being on the isle of Patmos (Revelation 1:9), to which he was probably banished during the wave of Christian persecution under the emperor Domitian. In 1831, the Prophet Joseph Smith indicated that John was then laboring among the lost ten tribes to prepare them for their return. (See Smith, *History of the Church*, 1:176.)

Revelation, chapters 1–3, deal mainly with John's day (although verses 1–3 of chapter 1 certainly deal with our day). Chapters 4–22 deal mainly with the future, including our day, and include glimpses back into premortality, as well as visions of the last days, the Second Coming, the Millennium, and celestial glory.

Symbolism

The use of symbolism in the book of Revelation is one of several things that make it hard to understand. While we use much symbolism in our own culture, the symbolism used by John is difficult for us to grasp, because we are not familiar with the culture of his day.

One of the great things about symbolism is that it is infinitely deep, meaning that through symbolism, the Holy Ghost can teach you one thing during one reading of a verse or set of verses, and then the next time you read it, you can be given a different message. For instance, suppose you are reading Revelation 1:18 where the Savior says, "I . . . have the keys of hell and of death." The symbolism used is "keys," meaning the power to lock or unlock, to condemn or set free. While you are reading this verse, the Holy Ghost impresses your mind that the Savior is our final Judge and can, if necessary, smite wicked people and transfer them to hell in order to cleanse the earth and free it from their wicked influence. Thus, in your heart, you say to yourself, "I'd better be good!" However, the next time you read this verse, with its symbolism of "the keys of hell and of death," your mind is on personal progress and improvement. This time, the Holy Ghost whispers that the Savior has the keys, through His Atonement, to free you from hell and from spiritual death. Thus, you are impressed and encouraged to repent and accept the cleansing and healing power of the Atonement in your own life.

The following list of symbols can be helpful to us in understanding the scriptures:

Symbolism Often Used in the Scriptures

Colors

white   purity; righteousness; exaltation (Example: Rev. 3:4–5)

black   evil; famine; darkness (Example: Rev. 6:5–6)

red   sins; bloodshed (Example: Rev. 6:4; D&C 133:51)

blue   heaven; godliness; remembering and keeping God's commandments (Example: Numbers 15:37–40)

green   life; nature (Example: Rev. 8:7)

amber   sun; light; divine glory (Example: D&C 110:2; Rev. 1:15; Ezek. 1:4, 27; 8:2)

scarlet   royalty (Example: Dan. 5:29; Matt. 27:28–29)

silver   worth, but less than gold (Example: Ridges, *Isaiah Made Easier*, Isa. 48:10 notes)

gold   the best; exaltation (Example: Rev. 4:4)

BODY PARTS

eye   perception; light and knowledge

head   governing

ears   obedience; hearing

mouth   speaking

hair   modesty; covering

members   offices and callings

heart   inner man; courage

hands   action, acting

right hand covenant hand; making covenants

bowels   center of emotion; whole being

loins   posterity; preparing for action (gird up your loins)

liver   center of feeling

reins   kidneys; center of desires, thoughts

arm   power

foot	mobility; foundation
toe	associated with cleansing rites (Example: Lev. 14:17)
nose	anger (Example: 2 Sam. 22:16; Job 4:9)
tongue	speaking
blood	life of the body
knee	humility; submission
shoulder	strength; effort
forehead	total dedication, loyalty (Example: Rev. 14:1 loyalty to God; Rev. 13:16 loyalty to wickedness, Satan)

NUMBERS

1	unity; God
3	God; Godhead; a word repeated three times means superlative, "the most," or "the best." (See Isa. 6:3.)
4	mankind; earth (See *Smith's Bible Dictionary*, p. 456.) (Example: Rev. 7:1, four angels over four parts of the earth)
7	completeness; perfection. When man lets God help, it leads to perfection. 4 + 3 = 7 (man + God = perfection)
10	numerical perfection; well-organized (Example: Ten Commandments, tithing) (Example: Satan is well-organized, Rev. 13:1)
12	divine government; God's organization (Example: JST, Rev. 5:6)
40 days	literal; sometimes means "a long time" as in 1 Sam. 17:16
forever	endless; can sometimes be a specific period or age, not endless (See *BYU Religious Studies Center Newsletter*, Vol. 8, No. 3, May 1994.)

OTHER

horse   victory; power to conquer (Example: Rev. 19:11; Jer. 8:16)

donkey   peace (Example: Christ came in peace at the Triumphal Entry)

palms   joy; triumph, victory (Example: John 12:13; Rev. 7:9)

wings   power to move, act, etc. (Example: Rev. 4:8; D&C 77:4)

crown   power; dominion; exaltation (Example: Rev. 2:10; 4:4)

robes   royalty; kings, queens; exaltation (Example: Rev. 6:11, 7:14; 2 Ne. 9:14; D&C 109:76; 3 Ne. 11:8)

REVELATION 1

As mentioned in the introductory material above, chapters 1–3 deal mainly with things in John's day, while chapters 4–22 deal mainly with the future. As you will see, the Joseph Smith Translation of the Bible (JST) is a great help to us in understanding this chapter. (Please read the note in the front of this study guide regarding the sources of JST quotes used in this work.) We will now proceed to verse 1 as it appears in our English Bible, followed by the Joseph Smith Translation of that verse.

1 The Revelation of Jesus Christ, which God gave unto him, to show unto his servants things which must shortly come to pass; and he sent and signified it by his angel unto his servant John:

JST Revelation 1:1

1 The Revelation of John, a servant of God, which was given unto him of Jesus Christ, to show unto his servants things which must shortly come to pass, that he sent and signified by his angel unto his servant John. [*This is an example of what is known as "divine investiture" where, in this case, an angel speaks directly for Christ as further clarified in Revelation 19:9–10.*]

Joseph Smith explained the phrase "which must shortly come to pass" in verse 1, above. He taught: "The things which John saw had no allusion to the scenes of the days of Adam, Enoch, Abraham or Jesus, only so far as is plainly represented by John, and clearly set forth by him. John saw that only which was lying in futurity and which was shortly to come to pass. See Revelation 1:1–3, which is a key to the whole subject" (Smith, *TPJS*, p. 289).

Divine Investiture

Let's take a moment here to say a bit more about divine investiture as mentioned in the note at the end of JST, verse 1, above. Often in the scriptures, without so indicating, the Savior speaks for the Father (example: D&C 29:1, 42, 46), the Holy Ghost speaks for the Savior (example: Moses 5:9), an angel speaks for the Savior (example: Revelation 1:1), and so forth. This is known as "divine investiture." Apostle Joseph Fielding Smith explained this divine investiture of authority as follows: "In giving revelations our Savior speaks at times for himself; at other times for the Father, and in the Father's name, as though he were the Father, and yet it is Jesus Christ, our Redeemer who gives the message. So, we see, in Doctrine and Covenants 29:1, that he introduces himself as 'Jesus Christ, your Redeemer,' but in the closing part of the revelation he speaks for the Father, and in the Father's name as though he were the Father, and yet it is still Jesus who is speaking, for the Father has put his name on him for that purpose" (Smith, *Doctrines of Salvation*, 1:27).

Apostle Jeffrey R. Holland also explained divine investiture: "Christ can at any time and in any place speak and act for the Father by virtue of the 'divine investiture of authority' the Father has given him" (Holland, *Christ and the New Covenant: The Messianic Message of the Book of Mormon*, pp. 183–84).

2 Who [*John*] bare record of the word of God, and of the testimony of Jesus Christ, and of all things that he [*John*] saw.

JST Revelation 1:2

2 Who bore record of the word of God, and of the testimony of Jesus Christ, and of all things that he saw.

3 Blessed is he that readeth, and they that hear the words of this prophecy [*the whole book of Revelation*], and keep those things which are written therein: for the time is at hand.

JST Revelation 1:3

3 Blessed are they who read, and they who hear and understand the words of this prophecy, and keep those things which are written therein, for the time of the coming of the Lord draweth nigh.

Did you notice that, according to the JST, above, John is addressing those of us who live in the last days when the Second Coming of the Savior is drawing near? He encourages us to understand and heed his writings, which contain much concerning conditions in the last days leading up to Christ's Coming.

4 John to the seven churches [*to the leaders of the seven "wards" or "branches" of the Church*] which are in Asia [*modern day western Turkey*]: Grace be unto you, and peace, from him [*Christ*] which is, and which was, and which is to come; and from the seven Spirits which are before his throne;

JST Revelation 1:4

4 Now this is the testimony of John to the seven servants

who are over the seven churches in Asia. Grace unto you, and peace from him who is, and who was, and who is to come; who hath sent forth his angel from before his throne, to testify unto those who are the seven servants over the seven churches [*the seven leaders, perhaps bishops or branch presidents who lead the seven Church units in what is now western Turkey*].

5 And from Jesus Christ, who is the faithful witness, and the first begotten of the dead [*the first resurrected*], and the prince of [*the leader over*] the kings of the earth. [*The JST puts the rest of verse 5 with verse 6.*] Unto him [*Christ*] that loved us, and washed us from our sins in his own blood [*the Atonement*],

JST Revelation 1:5

5 Therefore, I, John, the faithful witness, bear record of the things which were delivered me of the angel, and from Jesus Christ the first begotten of the dead, and the Prince of the kings of the earth.

The phrase "washed us from our sins in his own blood" in verse 5, above, and in JST verse 6 is symbolic of being cleansed by the Atonement.

It is interesting to note the cleansing role of blood in our own physical bodies. It constantly cleans out the toxins from each individual cell, and thus continually gives newness of life to each cell.

6 And hath made us kings and priests [*terms meaning exaltation*] unto God [*Heavenly Father, see JST, next*] and his Father; to him be glory and dominion for ever and ever. Amen.

Next, in JST 1:6, John testifies that we can be exalted because of the cleansing that is available to us through the Atonement of Christ.

JST Revelation 1:6

6 And unto him who loved us, be glory; who washed us from our sins in his own blood, and hath made us kings and priests unto God, his Father. To him be glory and dominion, for ever and ever. Amen.

Bruce R. McConkie explains verse 6, above, as follows: "If righteous men have power through the gospel and its crowning ordinance of celestial marriage to become kings and priests to rule in exaltation forever, it follows that the women by their side (without whom they cannot attain exaltation) will be queens and priestesses (Revelation 1:6; 5:10). Exaltation grows out of the eternal union of a man and his wife. Of those whose marriage endures in eternity, the Lord says, 'Then shall they be gods' (D&C 132:20); that is, each of them, the man and the woman, will be a god. As such they will rule over their dominions forever" (McConkie, *Mormon Doctrine*, p. 613).

Next, John gives us some details of the Second Coming.

7 Behold, he [*Christ*] cometh with clouds [*symbolic of the presence of the Lord; see Exodus 13:21 and Exodus 19:9*]; and every eye shall see him, and they also which pierced him [*even those who participated in his crucifixion will see Him at the Second Coming; see quote from Orson Pratt, below*]: and all kindreds [*the wicked*] of the earth shall wail because of him. Even so, Amen.

JST Revelation 1:7

7 For behold, he cometh in the clouds with ten thousands of his saints in the kingdom, clothed with the glory of his Father. And every eye shall see him; and they who pierced him, and all kindreds of the earth shall wail because of him. Even so, Amen.

Apostle Orson Pratt explained verse 7, above, as follows: "Jesus will come in a cloud, or as is expressed here in the 40th chapter of Isaiah—'The glory of the Lord will be revealed and all flesh shall see it together.' It is also expressed in the revelations of St. John, that when he comes in a cloud every eye shall see him, and they also which pierced him. It seems then that the second advent of the Son of God is to be something altogether of a different nature from anything that has hitherto transpired on the face of the earth, accompanied with great power and glory, something that will not be done in a small portion of the earth like Palestine, and seen only by a few; but it will be an event that will be seen by all—all flesh shall see the glory of the Lord; when he reveals himself the second time, every eye, not only those living at that time in the flesh, in mortality on the earth, but also the very dead themselves, they also who pierced him, those who lived eighteen hundred years ago, who were engaged in the cruel act of piercing his hands and his feet and his side, will also see him at that time" (Pratt, *Journal of Discourses,* 18:171).

8 I am Alpha and Omega [*the beginning and ending letters of the Greek alphabet*], the beginning and the ending, saith the Lord, which is, and which was, and which is to come, the Almighty. [*In other words, I have been involved with you since the beginning, premortality, and creation, and I will be around at the end of the earth as I judge you and finish all things the Father has asked Me to do.*]

JST Revelation 1:8

8 For he saith, I am Alpha and Omega, the beginning and the ending, the Lord, who is, and who was, and who is to come, the Almighty.

Having set the stage now, John proceeds to tell us what the circumstances in his life were at the time he received this revelation.

9 I John [*the Beloved Apostle*], who also am your brother, and companion in tribulation [*I've got problems too; I understand you*], and in the kingdom and patience of Jesus Christ, was in the isle that is called Patmos [*He was banished to Patmos, an island just off the west coast of Turkey, just below the island of Samos. For the location of Samos, see E2 on map 13 of your Bible, or D2 on map 22 in the 1989 LDS Bible. Put a dot on your map just under Samos and label it Patmos.*], for the word of God, and for the testimony of Jesus Christ. [*I am banished because I wouldn't stop teaching and living the gospel.*]

10 I was in the Spirit on the Lord's day [*Sunday, Acts 20:7*], and heard behind me a great voice, as of a trumpet,

Trumpet is used often in the scriptures to represent a clear, easy-to-recognize message from God, just as a trumpet is a clear, easy-to-recognize musical instrument for us today.

Revelation 19:10 informs us that an angel is speaking for Jesus Christ here. As mentioned earlier, this is known as "divine investiture."

11 Saying, I [*Christ*] am Alpha and Omega, the first and the last: and, What thou seest, write in a book, and send it unto the seven churches [*"wards" or "branches"*] which are in Asia [*western Turkey today*]; unto Ephesus, and unto Smyrna, and unto Pergamos, and unto Thyatira, and unto Sardis, and unto Philadelphia, and unto Laodicea [*these seven cities are listed in geographical order*].

12 And I turned to see the voice

that spake with me. And being turned, I saw seven golden candlesticks [*representing the seven "wards" or "branches"*];

Symbolism is involved here and carries an important message. Gold symbolizes the best, or the true gospel. Candlesticks do not give light, rather, they carry the source of light, which is Christ and His gospel, to the world.

JST Revelation 1:12

12 And I turned to see from whence the voice came that spake to me; and being turned, I saw seven golden candlesticks;

13 And in the midst [*D&C 38:7 reminds us that Christ is often in our midst*] of the seven candlesticks one like unto the Son of man [*Christ*], clothed with a garment down to the foot, and girt about the paps [*breast, chest*] with a golden [*symbolic of the best; celestial*] girdle.

The phrase "one like unto the Son of man" in verse 13, above, needs explaining. The question is, why don't they just say "Jesus Christ" rather than using an oblique reference to Him? Answer: In order to keep the commandment "Thou shalt not take the name of the Lord

thy God in vain" (Exodus 20:7), the Jews developed rules and standard practices that kept them far away from taking the name of the Lord in vain. For instance, rather than saying the Lord's name directly, they would use an indirect reference such as "one like unto," and then the name. Thus, they avoided even coming close to breaking the commandment. Many examples of this practice show reverence and respect toward the name of Deity. For instance, see Daniel 3:25, 7:13; Revelation 14:14; Abraham 3:27; and 1 Nephi 1:8.

The phrase "Son of man," in reference to Christ in verse 13, above, and elsewhere in the scriptures is explained in Moses 6:57 as follows: "In the language of Adam, Man of Holiness is his name, and the name of his Only Begotten is the Son of Man, even Jesus Christ." In other words, "Man of Holiness" refers to Heavenly Father. Jesus is, therefore, the "Son of Man of Holiness," which, in the Bible, is shortened to "Son of man."

14 His head and his hairs were white like wool, as white as snow; and his eyes were as a flame of fire [*this is similar to the description of the Savior in D&C 110:3*];

It is interesting to notice that the word "wool" and the phrase "white as snow," used in verse 14, above, are also used in Isaiah 1:18 in describing the power of the Atonement to cleanse and heal from sin. Isaiah 1:18 says, "Come now, and let us reason together, saith the LORD: though your sins be as scarlet, they shall be as white as snow; though they be red like crimson, they shall be as wool." The use here is no doubt a tie-in with Isaiah 1:18 and a reminder to us of the power of the Atonement.

15 And his feet like unto fine brass, as if they burned in a furnace; and his voice as the sound of many waters.

16 And he had in his right hand [*covenant hand, see symbolism sheet at the beginning of this study guide*] seven stars [*the leaders of the seven "wards" or "branches"; stars are symbolical. We rely on them, like we rely on our Church leaders, to guide us through darkness to our desired destination.*]: and out of his [*Christ's*] mouth went a sharp twoedged sword [*Perhaps symbolical of the fact that the Savior can both defend the righteous and destroy the wicked; see 2:16. It is our choice. Also, a two-edged sword, representing*

the word of God as in JST, Revelation 19:15, can cut quickly through falsehood and error.]: and his countenance was as the sun shineth in his strength.

JST Revelation 1:16

16 And he had in his right hand seven stars; and out of his mouth went a sharp two-edged sword; and his countenance was as the sun shining in his strength.

Next, in verse 17, John tells us how seeing the resurrected Savior (see heading to this chapter in your Bible) affected him at this moment.

17 And when I [*John*] saw him, I fell at his feet as dead [*completely overwhelmed*]. And he laid his right hand [*covenant hand; symbolizing that via making and keeping covenants we can feel at ease in Christ's presence*] upon me, saying unto me, Fear not; I am the first and the last [*I am Jesus Christ your Savior; you don't need to be afraid of Me.*]:

18 I am he that liveth, and was dead [*I have been literally resurrected!*]; and, behold, I am alive for evermore [*I will continue to live forever.*], Amen; and have the keys of hell and of death. [*I overcame all things and thus*

have all power to save you; I can redeem you from spiritual death as well as physical death; I am fully qualified to be your Savior.]

19 Write the things which thou hast seen, and the things which are, and the things which shall be hereafter [*write this vision down*];

> The angel, speaking for Christ, now explains to John some of the imagery used so far in the vision.

20 The mystery [*meaning*] of the seven stars which thou sawest in my right hand, and the seven golden candlesticks. The seven stars are the angels of the seven churches [*the leaders of the seven wards or branches*]: and the seven candlesticks which thou sawest are the seven churches [*the seven wards or branches*].

JST Revelation 1:20

20 This is the mystery of the seven stars which thou sawest in my right hand, and the seven golden candlesticks. The seven stars are the servants [*leaders, presiding elders*] of the seven churches; and the seven candlesticks which thou sawest are the seven churches.

REVELATION 2

The Savior here and in chapter 3 gives personal messages through John the Revelator to the Saints of his day in the various "wards" or "branches" spoken of in Revelation 1:11, which were located in what is known as western Turkey today. Notice the symbolism representing the celestial kingdom at the end of each of these messages. Watch for counsel about how to faithfully live the gospel and for warnings that can help us avoid leaving the path that leads to exaltation.

The first message in this chapter is the Savior's message to the members of the Ephesus "ward" or "branch" in verses 1–7, next.

One of the first things we see is that the Savior tenderly helps His bishops and branch presidents as they strive to nourish the members of their wards and branches. We also see that He is often present among the members of His Church. Perhaps you have felt His presence on such special occasions.

1 Unto the angel [*presiding elder, leader*] of the church ["*ward*"] of Ephesus write; These things saith he [*Christ*] that holdeth the seven stars ["*branch presidents*"

or "bishops"; the Savior simi-
larly helps our Church leaders
today] in his right hand [covenant
hand], who walketh in the midst
of the seven golden candlesticks
[the seven wards or branches; the
Savior is in our midst, D&C 38:7;
He is not an absentee Savior];

JST Revelation 2:1

1 Unto the servant of the church
of Ephesus write; These things
saith he that holdeth the seven
stars in his right hand, who
walketh in the midst of the
seven golden candlesticks;

In the next few verses, the
Savior will first compliment
these Church members and
then express some concerns
to them. There is a lesson to be
learned here from the Master
Teacher regarding appropriate
and effective parenting and
leadership. Where possible,
compliment and encourage
before expressing concerns
and disciplining.

2 I know thy works, and thy
labour, and thy patience [you
have done much good and have
exemplified many Christlike qual-
ities], and how thou canst not bear
them which are evil [you are not
passive about evil when it comes
among you]: and thou hast tried
[tested] them which say they are

apostles, and are not, and hast
found them liars [you have faced
issues and dealt properly with
apostates among you];

3 And hast born, and hast
patience, and for my name's sake
hast laboured, and hast not fainted
[you haven't given up living the
gospel when the going was dif-
ficult].

4 Nevertheless I have somewhat
against thee [I have a serious
concern], because thou hast left
thy first love [your enthusiasm
for the gospel when you were first
converted; now you are diminish-
ing in zeal and getting weak in
the faith].

5 Remember therefore from
whence thou art fallen, and repent,
and do the first works [return to
your former level of commitment
and enthusiasm]; or else I will
come unto thee quickly, and will
remove thy candlestick out of his
place, except thou repent [your
"ward" will die out much faster
than you might think possible, if
you don't repent].

The advice given to the members of the Ephesus Ward in
verses 4 and 5, above, is vital
counsel for all of us. We must
avoid becoming apathetic and
sloppy in our commitment to the

Lord the longer we are members of the Church. A reminder phrase we see often in the scriptures, in one form or another is "endure faithfully to the end."

6 But this thou hast [*here is another compliment, something you are doing right*], that thou hatest the deeds of the Nicolaitans [*D&C 117:11; people who want the prestige of Church membership but who are not fully committed to the gospel; they secretly want to follow the ways of the world*], which I also hate.

Next, in verse 7, you will see a phrase that is used often in this chapter and the next. It is "He that hath an ear let him hear." It is an important phrase for all of us. It means that all who are willing to pay attention to the promptings of the Spirit and follow them must do so in order to receive the available guidance and blessings.

7 He that hath an ear, let him hear what the Spirit saith unto the churches [*listen carefully to the promptings of the Holy Ghost, who teaches and warns members of the Church constantly*]; To him that overcometh will I give to eat of the tree of life, which is in the midst of the paradise of God. [*Celestial glory is the reward of*

the righteous. Perhaps this counsel to the Ephesus Saints reflects upon the tree of life found in Lehi's dream in 1 Nephi 8. Also note that the Nicolaitans in verse 6 of Revelation 2 seem to tie in with the "great and spacious building" in 1 Nephi 8:26–27, while verse 5, above, might tie in with 1 Nephi 8:25, where members have tasted the gospel but then let peer pressure make them ashamed of it, which results in their letting go of the iron rod.]

Next, the Savior gives John a message for the Saints in Smyrna.

8 And unto the angel [*presiding elder*] of the church ["*ward*"] in Smyrna write; These things saith the first and the last [*the Savior*], which was dead, and is alive [*is resurrected*];

JST Revelation 2:8

8 And unto the servant of the church in Smyrna write; These things saith the first and the last, which was dead, and is alive;

9 I know thy works, and tribulation, and poverty (but thou art rich) [*you are well-off because you have the gospel*] and I know the blasphemy [*sacrilegious*

thinking and behavior; perhaps referring here to the slanderous false accusations of the Jews in Smyrna who are persecuting the Saints there] of them which say they are Jews [*who claim to be "the chosen people of the Lord"*], and are not [*they are not faithful and have rejected Christ and are persecuting the Saints in Smyrna*], but are the synagogue of Satan [*the church of the devil; 1 Nephi 14:10; 1 Nephi 13:6–9*].

10 Fear none of those things which thou shalt suffer [*you will have some suffering as part of your "curriculum" here on earth, but don't fear it*]: behold, the devil shall cast some of you into prison [*literally, in Smyrna, by wicked Jewish leaders and the Romans; figuratively, Satan constantly strives to limit or prevent our progress in the gospel*], that ye may be tried [*tested*]; and ye shall have tribulation ten days [*perhaps meaning a short time compared to eternity; this might appropriately compare to Daniel 1:12 and 14 where Daniel and his companions are "proved" for ten days*]: be thou faithful unto death [*endure to the end*], and I will give thee a crown of life [*you will be a god in exaltation; see D&C 124:55; 132:19–20*].

11 He that hath an ear [*he who is willing to listen*], let him hear what the Spirit saith unto the churches; He that overcometh [*who overcomes evil through the Atonement of Christ*] shall not be hurt of the second death [*will not suffer spiritual death and be cut off from the presence of God forever; in other words, you will receive a celestial reward*].

Just a word about the term "second death," as used in verse 11, above. In this context, it means to be permanently cut off from returning to the direct presence of God in celestial glory. John defines some lifestyles that could lead to second death or spiritual death, later in his revelation.

Revelation 21:8

8 But the fearful, and unbelieving, and the abominable, and murderers, and whoremongers, and sorcerers, and idolaters, and all liars, shall have their part in the lake which burneth with fire and brimstone: which is the second death.

"Spiritual death" is often used synonymously with "second death" in the scriptures. Example: Alma 12:16. In the *Gospel Principles* manual, page 29, spiritual death is explained as follows: "Because of their transgression, Adam and Eve also suffered spiritual death. This meant they and their children could not walk and talk face to face with God. Adam and Eve and their children were separated from God both physically and spiritually."

The next message from the Savior goes to the Saints living in Pergamos. One of the comforting messages we can gain here is the assurance that the Lord is completely aware of our circumstances. You will see that one of the faithful members of the Church has given his life for the gospel. Once again, we will see compliments given and concerns expressed by the Savior.

12 And to the angel [*leader*] of the church ["*ward*"] in Pergamos [*a center for Roman emperor worship*] write; These things saith he [*Christ*] which hath the sharp sword with two edges [*Revelation 1:16*];

JST Revelation 2:12

12 And to the servant of the church in Pergamos write; These things saith he which hath the sharp sword with two edges;

13 I know thy works, and where thou dwellest [*I know your situation*], even where Satan's seat is

[*you live in an area where evil and false religions are very strong*]: and thou holdest fast my name [*and you are remaining faithful to the covenants you made when you took My name upon you*], and hast not denied my faith [*a compliment*], even in those days wherein Antipas was my faithful martyr [*gave his life for the gospel*], who was slain among you, where Satan dwelleth [*where Satan has great power over many*].

Among other things in verse 14, next, you will see a reference to a man named Balaam in the Old Testament. You may remember that Balaam's donkey refused to go where he wanted to ride, crushed his foot against a wall (Numbers 22:25), lay down with him still trying to ride her, and started talking to him (Numbers 22:26–34).

It helps here to know that Moab was a nation located east of the Dead Sea and was in the path of the children of Israel as they journeyed toward the promised land. Balak, king of Moab (spelled "Balac" here in Revelation in the New Testament), attempted several times to hire or bribe Balaam to use his priesthood to curse the approaching children of Israel to prevent them from destroying

Moab. Balaam knew that the priesthood should not be used this way (In fact, it cannot be used this way. See D&C 121:36–37.), especially to curse the people of the Lord, but he was sorely tempted to endeavor to use his priesthood for the wealth, potential honor, and fame offered him by the king of Moab (Numbers 22–24).

Ultimately, Balaam tried to do an end run around the instructions of the Lord. He told Balak, king of Moab, that he could not curse the Israelites because of the word of the Lord to him, but if Balak would get his people to entice the Israelites to get involved with idol worship and the accompanying sexual immorality, they would lose the blessings of the Lord and thus would no longer be a threat to the Moabites (see Numbers 31:16). This misguided and wicked counsel of Balaam to Balak is referred to next in verse 14.

14 But I have a few things against thee [*I have some concerns about you*], because thou hast there them that hold the doctrine of Balaam [*priestcraft; preaching for popularity, money, and approval of men; see Numbers 22; 2 Nephi 26:29*], who taught Balac to cast a stumblingblock before the children of Israel, to eat things sacrificed unto idols [*participating in idol worship*], and to commit fornication [*sexual immorality, including that used as part of idol worship in many Bible cults; "fornication" can also mean breaking covenants, intense and total disloyalty to God. See Jeremiah 3:8 and Revelation 14:8; also see Bible Dictionary under "Adultery"*].

15 So hast thou also them that hold the doctrine of the Nicolaitans [*some members of the Church in your area are thinking like Nicolaitans; see verse 6, above*], which thing I hate.

16 Repent; or else I will come unto thee quickly, and will fight against them with the sword of my mouth [*the two-edged sword referred to in 1:16 can destroy the wicked as well as protect the righteous*].

17 He that hath an ear [*who is spiritually in tune*], let him hear what the Spirit saith unto the churches; To him that overcometh [*who overcomes sin and evil through repentance and the Atonement*] will I give to eat of the hidden manna [*nourishment from heaven*], and will give him a white stone [*symbolic of celestial*

glory, *D&C 130:11*], and in the stone a new name [*symbolic of celestial glory; see also Revelation 3:12*] written, which no man knoweth saving he that receiveth it [*a key word, D&C 130:11*].

JST Revelation 2:17

17 He that hath an ear, let him hear what the Spirit saith unto the churches; To him that overcometh will I give to eat of the hidden manna, and will give him a white stone, and in the stone a new name written, which no man knowest saving he that receiveth it.

Isaiah mentions "a new name, which the mouth of the Lord shall name" in Isaiah 62:2. Additional information about the term "new name," as used in verse 17, above, is given in the Doctrine and Covenants. According to D&C 130:10–11, a "white stone" is given to each of those who attains the celestial kingdom. In D&C 130:11, the "new name" is referred to as "the key word" and is used in conjunction with celestial glory and exaltation.

Brigham Young explained the term "key word" in conjunction with temple endowments as follows: "Your endowment is to receive all those ordinances in the house of the Lord, which are necessary for you, after you have departed this life, to enable you to walk back to the presence of the Father, passing the angels who stand as sentinels, being enabled to give them the key words, the signs and tokens, pertaining to the holy Priesthood, and gain your eternal exaltation in spite of earth and hell" (Young, *Discourses of Brigham Young*, p. 416).

It is interesting to note that people anciently had new names given them upon making additional covenants with the Lord. Examples include Abram, whose name was changed to Abraham when he made covenants of exaltation with the Lord (Genesis 17:5). In the heading to JST, Genesis 17, the term "new name" appears again as "Abram's new name." Likewise, Sarai's name was changed to Sarah (Genesis 17:15–16), Jacob's name was changed to Israel (Genesis 32:28), and Saul's name was changed to Paul (Acts 13:2–3, 9 and 13).

King Mosiah promised his people another name if they would be diligent "in keeping the commandments of the Lord" (Mosiah 1:11). The name he gave them was the name of Jesus Christ (Mosiah 5:8 and 11), which is the name through which we receive exaltation if worthy. (See Mosiah 5:7.)

Robert L. Millet spoke of this name that King Benjamin gave his people as follows: "As members of the family of Christ, they were required to take upon them a new name, the name of Christ; they thereby became Christians in the truest sense of the word and were obligated by covenant to live by the rules and regulations of the royal family, to live a life befitting the new and sacred name they had taken" (Millet, *Alive in Christ: The Miracle of Spiritual Rebirth*, p. 77).

Next, the Lord gives John a message for the members in Thyatira.

18 And unto the angel [*leader*] of the church in Thyatira write; These things saith the Son of God, who hath his eyes like unto a flame of fire, and his feet are like fine brass;

JST Revelation 2:18

18 And unto the servant of the church in Thyatira write; These things saith the Son of God, who hath his eyes like unto a flame of fire, and his feet are like fine brass;

19 I know thy works, and charity, and service, and faith, and thy patience, and thy works [*a compliment*]; and the last to be more than the first. [*In effect, your recent works are greater than your previous works; one possible meaning might be that these members are continuing to progress in living the gospel.*]

As you will see next in verses 20–22, the Savior has a very serious concern about some of the members and leaders of the Church in Thyatira. It can remind us of our day and age where many evil forces are encouraging us to be more tolerant of lifestyles that involve sexual immorality and many varieties of apostate living.

20 [*A concern:*] Notwithstanding I have a few things against thee, because thou sufferest [*you allow*] that woman Jezebel, which calleth herself a prophetess, to teach [*Major message: There are limits as to what you can tolerate in the Church. You leaders should not allow her to do this teaching in your congregation.*] and to seduce my servants to commit fornication [*can be literal, referring to various forms of sexual immorality; can*

also mean apostasy, total disloyalty—see Revelation 14:8; Bible Dictionary under "Adultery"], and to eat things sacrificed unto idols [*in other words, participating in idol worship*].

Note one of the very comforting doctrines of the gospel as exemplified in verse 21, next. It is that the Lord is anxious to give us the opportunity to repent (for example, see Mosiah 26:30). Apparently, Jezebel has been given many opportunities.

Note that the JST verse that follows indicates that she has been involved in multiple cases of sexual immorality.

21 And I gave her space to repent of her fornication [*she had plenty of chances to repent*]; and she repented not.

JST Revelation 2:21

21 And I gave her space to repent of her fornications; and she repented not.

Note how vital the JST changes are for verse 22, next!

22 Behold, I will cast her into a bed, and them [*her followers*] that commit adultery [*could also symbolically mean those who have joined her in apostasy*] with

her into great tribulation, except [*unless*] they repent of their deeds.

JST Revelation 2:22

22 Behold, I will cast her into hell, and them that commit adultery with her into great tribulation, except they repent of their deeds.

Next, in verse 23, we see that gross wickedness and violation of covenants can lead to spiritual death. Remember that these people were members of the Church in John's day. Thus, they would have made covenants with God, which they were violating by their choice to follow Jezebel's teachings.

23 And I will kill her children [*followers*] with death [*spiritual death*]; and all the churches [*"wards"*] shall know that I am he which searcheth [*knows*] the reins [*literally kidneys, loins; symbolically the center of thoughts and desires; in other words, the inner person*] and hearts: and I will give unto every one of you according to your works.

Next, in verse 24, we are informed that there were many in the Thyatira Ward who were doing their best to live the gospel.

24 But unto you [*the presiding*

officer] I say, and unto the rest in Thyatira, as many as have not this doctrine [*who haven't become followers of Jezebel*], and which have not known the depths of Satan [*haven't gone deep into apostasy*], as they speak; I will put upon you none other burden [*I will not express any other concerns about you at this time; just work on this one*].

Did you notice another important principle at the end of verse 24, above? It is that the Savior does not expect us to achieve perfection overnight, so to speak. Rather, He gives us things to work on in our lives, and when we finally do well enough with them, He will give us additional things to work on. If we do not understand this principle, it would be quite easy to become overwhelmed trying to live the gospel.

25 But that which ye have already [*the things in which you are being faithful*] hold fast till I come [*endure to the end*].

Many people of other religions take strong offense at the teachings of our Church that faithful members can attain exaltation and actually become gods. Such individuals obviously have not carefully read

or have not understood what John recorded in these next verses. As you read verses 26–28, you will find this doctrine clearly taught. You will also see that the wicked are destroyed because they break the commandments of God.

26 And he that overcometh, and keepeth my works unto the end [*he who overcomes evil through faith in Christ and keeps His commandments*], to him will I give power over the nations [*celestial reward; in other words, such individuals will become gods and will rule over their own worlds; D&C 132:20*]:

JST Revelation 2:26

26 And to him who overcometh, and keepeth my commandments unto the end, will I give power over many kingdoms;

27 And he [*those who overcome all things*] shall rule them [*nations, future worlds; D&C 132:20*] with a rod of iron [*the word of God— see JST below; also, 1 Nephi 11:25*]; as the vessels [*clay pots*] of a potter shall they be broken to shivers [*broken to bits, if they are disobedient*]: even as I received of my Father [*just as is the case with Me and My work on this earth*].

24 THE BOOK OF REVELATION MADE EASIER

JST Revelation 2:27

27 And he shall rule them with the word of God; and they shall be in his hands as the vessels of clay in the hands of a potter; and he shall govern them by faith, with equity and justice, even as I received of my Father.

28 And I will give him [*the righteous in verses 26–27*] the morning star [*the brightest, best; symbolic of exaltation*].

29 He that hath an ear, let him hear what the Spirit saith unto the churches [*pay close attention and obey what I say to you through the Holy Ghost*].

REVELATION 3

As the vision continues, John is given messages from the Savior to three more units of the Church in what is known as western Turkey today, namely Sardis, Philadelphia, and Laodicea. Among other things in this chapter, we are taught about the book of life (verse 5) and again, the fact that worthy people can become gods (verse 21).

1 And unto the angel [*presiding officer*] of the church [*"ward"*] in Sardis write; These things saith he [*the Savior*] that hath the seven Spirits of God, and the seven stars [*JST, "the seven stars, which are the seven servants of God," i.e., I'm holding the seven "bishops" of the seven "wards" in the hollow of My hand; I am directing them*]; I know thy works, that thou hast a name that thou livest [*you have a reputation for being good*], and art dead [*see JST change below*].

JST Revelation 3:1

1 And unto the servant of the church in Sardis, write; These things saith he who hath the seven stars, which are the seven servants of God [*in other words, the Savior is holding the seven "bishops" of the seven "wards" in the hollow of His hand; He is directing them*]; I know thy works, that thou hast a name that thou livest, and art not dead [*in effect, you still have some spirituality left—see verse 2, next*].

2 Be watchful, and strengthen the things which remain, that are ready to die: for I have not found thy works perfect before God. [*An understatement of concern!*]

JST Revelation 3:2

2 Be watchful therefore, and strengthen those who remain, who are ready to die [*spiritually*]; for I have not found thy works perfect before God.

3 Remember therefore how thou hast received and heard [*the gospel*], and hold fast [*keep your commitments*], and repent. If therefore thou shalt not watch, I will come on thee as a thief [*unexpectedly; Strong's, #2240*], and thou shalt not know what hour I will come upon thee.

The reference to *Strong's* #2240, in verse 3, above, refers to *Strong's Exhaustive Concordance of the Bible*, which is a reference book for Bible word definitions widely used by Bible scholars.

4 Thou hast a few names [*you have a few members*] even in Sardis which have not defiled their garments [*a compliment; you still have a few righteous members*]; and they shall walk with me in white [*symbolic of exaltation*]: for they are worthy.

You may wish to refer back to the symbolism section of this study guide near the front of the book and study some of the color symbolism used in the scriptures.

5 He that overcometh [*he who overcomes sin through Christ's Atonement*], the same shall be clothed in white raiment [*white clothing; symbolic of exaltation*]; and I will not blot out his name out of the book of life, but I will confess [*acknowledge, praise*] his name before my Father [*as in D&C 45:3–5*], and before his angels [*they will receive celestial reward*].

The term "book of life" mentioned in verse 5, above, is referred to as the "Lamb's Book of Life" in D&C 132:19. It represents the records kept in heaven in which the names of those worthy of exaltation are written.

Bruce R. McConkie taught: "In a literal sense, the book of life, or Lamb's book of Life, is the record kept in heaven which contains the names of the faithful and an account of their righteous covenants and deeds. . . . The book of life is the book containing the names of those who shall inherit eternal life [exaltation] . . . it is the book of eternal life. It is "the book of the names of the sanctified, even them of the celestial world" (D&C 88:2; McConkie, *Mormon Doctrine*, p. 97).

6 He that hath an ear, let him hear what the Spirit saith unto the churches.

As you continue reading, notice that the message of the Savior to the members of the Church in Philadelphia contains only compliments.

7 And to the angel [*presiding officer*] of the church in Philadelphia write; These things saith he [*Christ*] that is holy, he that is true, he that hath the key of David [*mentioned in Isaiah 22:22; meaning, among other things, power to command and be obeyed; also can mean Christ, who holds the priesthood keys of exaltation*], he that openeth, and no man shutteth; and shutteth, and no man openeth [*Christ's Atonement can set us free from death and hell, in spite of Satan's efforts against us, or He, as our final Judge—see John 5:22—can condemn us on Judgment Day.*];

JST Revelation 3:7

7 And to the servant of the church in Philadelphia write; These things saith he that is holy, he that is true, he that hath the key of David, he that openeth, and no man shutteth; and shutteth, and no man openeth;

8 I know thy works: behold, I have set before thee an open door [*I have prepared the way for you to come unto Me*], and no man can shut it [*no man can stop you*]: for thou hast a little strength, and hast kept my word [*you are improving and you are keeping your commitments to Me*], and

hast not denied my name [*and you have not rejected Me*].

From verse 9, next, we see that the members of the Church in Philadelphia (located in what is western Turkey today) lived in an area where Satan had a stronghold among the inhabitants. In our world in these last days, we live in a similar environment.

9 Behold, I will make them of the synagogue of Satan [*the church of the devil, 1 Nephi 14:10; Revelation 2:9*], which say they are Jews, and are not [*who are in apostasy but still claim to be the Lord's covenant people*], but do lie [*in word as well as through their personal wickedness*]; behold, I will make them to come and worship before thy feet [*you will be exalted and have power over them when you become gods; see D&C 132:20*], and to know that I have loved thee [*I have been privileged to bless you because of your righteousness; see Nelson, "Divine Love," Ensign, Feb. 2003 pp. 20–25*].

Can you see that the promise in verse 9, above, that the enemies of the Church will someday bow down before faithful members, most likely will not be fulfilled during their lifetime?

However, faithful Saints will someday become gods (D&C 132:20) and at that point, the promise here will, in effect, be fulfilled. This principle can apply to patriarchal blessings. Some of the promises given in them may find fulfillment in the next life. Often, when an ordained patriarch lays his hands upon the head of the blessing's recipient, the line between mortality and eternity dissolves in the patriarch's mind and the blessing given from the Father under the hands of the patriarch moves into the "past, present, and future" realm in which the Father resides.

Next, in verse 10, the doctrine that this mortal life is designed to be a test for us, and that God helps faithful members pass it, is clearly taught.

10 Because thou hast kept the word of my patience [*you have patiently kept your commitments and covenants, Hebrews 10:36*], I also will keep thee from the hour of temptation [*will help and protect you during temptation*], which shall come upon all the world, to try [*test*] them that dwell upon the earth.

11 Behold, I come quickly [*not "soon"; rather, when I do come,*

it will be "quickly" (see Strong's, #5035) and the wicked will not have time to repent and escape]: hold that fast which thou hast [*keep your commitments and maintain your faithfulness*], that no man take thy crown [*symbolic of exaltation*].

Notice the various ways exaltation is described in verse 12, next. We will use **bold** to point them out.

12 Him that **overcometh** [*evil and wickedness through the Atonement of Christ*] will I make a **pillar in the temple of my God** [*you will receive exaltation in my temple; in other words, in the celestial kingdom; see Revelation 21:22*], and **he shall go no more out** [*exaltation lasts forever*]: and **I will write upon him the name of my God** [*symbolism meaning he will belong to God; in other words, exaltation; Revelation 14:1; 22:4*], **and the name of the city of my God, which is new Jerusalem** [*your eternal "address" will be "New Jerusalem, celestial kingdom"*], which cometh down out of heaven from my God: and I will write upon him my **new name** [*referred to in 2:17; symbolic of celestial glory, D&C 130:11*].

JST Revelation 3:12

12 Him that overcometh will I make a pillar in the temple of my God, and he shall go no more out; and I will write upon him the name of my God, and the name of the city of my God, this is New Jerusalem, which cometh down out of heaven from my God; and I will write upon him my new name.

The phrase "new name" has meaning understood only by endowed members of The Church of Jesus Christ of Latter-day Saints. See the note after Revelation 2:17 in this study guide.

13 He that hath an ear, let him hear what the Spirit saith unto the churches.

To this next "ward" or "branch" of the Church, the Savior expresses only concerns. From what Christ tells them, we should learn that one of the most serious concerns of all is indecision about whether or not to be completely committed to God.

By the way, have you noticed that in each of the Savior's introductions of Himself to the various "wards" or "branches" of the Church in chapters 2 and 3, He uses fascinating variety?

14 And unto the angel [*presiding officer*] of the church of the Laodiceans write; These things saith the Amen [*Christ*], the faithful and true witness [*Christ*], the beginning of the creation of God [*the Father; in other words, the firstborn spirit child of our Heavenly Father as mentioned in Colossians 1:15*];

JST Revelation 3:14

14 And unto the servant of the church of the Laodiceans write; These things saith the Amen, the faithful and true witness, the beginning of the creation of God;

15 I know thy works, that thou art neither cold nor hot [*you won't make a commitment or take a stand*]: I would [*wish that*] thou wert cold or hot.

16 So then because thou art lukewarm [*you won't make a solid commitment*], and neither cold nor hot, I will spue [*vomit; see Revelation 3:16, footnote b in our Bible*] thee out of my mouth [*I will reject you*].

17 Because thou sayest, I am rich, and increased with goods [*I have lots of worldly possessions; Strong's, #4147*], and have need of nothing [*you are materialistic*]; and knowest not that thou

art wretched, and miserable, and poor, and blind, and naked [*you don't realize how spiritually poor and destitute you really are!*]:

> Next, the Savior explains how such people can repent. This counsel applies to all of us.

18 I counsel thee to buy of me [*through repentance and renewed commitment*] gold [*symbolic of the best, the gospel, the Atonement, and ultimately exaltation*] tried in the fire [*refined; proven to be the best*], that thou mayest be [*truly*] rich; and white raiment [*buy white robes from Me, made available to you through My Atonement; symbolic of purity and exaltation*], that thou mayest be clothed, and that the shame of thy nakedness do not appear [*you need to repent and be clothed with righteousness, so you do not stand naked, or in other words, without excuse for your sins, and embarrassed on Judgment Day; see 2 Nephi 9:14*]; and anoint thine eyes [*prepare your spiritual eyes*] with eyesalve, that thou mayest see [*eye salve often hurts at first and then heals; so also with the Holy Ghost . . . it sometimes hurts at first, but when heeded, heals.*]

> Can you hear and feel the tender voice of our loving Savior explaining that it is

because of His perfect love for these wishy-washy members in Laodicea that He has chastised them?

> Note also that it is not too late for them. At the end of verse 19, He gives them an open invitation to repent.

19 As many as I love, I rebuke and chasten [*D&C 95:1*]: be zealous [*pursue the "gold" in verse 18 earnestly; Strong's, #2206*] therefore, and repent.

> Perhaps you have seen paintings depicting verse 20, next. If so, did you notice that the artist did not put a doorknob on the outside of the door? It is symbolic of the fact that the Savior knocks, but we must let Him into our hearts and lives.

20 Behold, I [*the Savior*] stand at the door [*your door; your life*], and knock [*waiting humbly for you to respond*]: if any man hear [*pay attention to*] my voice, and open the door [*we have the agency to or not to*], I will come in to him, and will sup [*eat the evening meal; can be symbolic of the Last Supper, the sacrament; in other words, making covenants*] with him, and he with me.

> "Throne," as used in verse 21,

next, symbolizes exaltation, or in other words, attaining the highest degree of glory in the celestial kingdom and becoming gods as described in D&C 132:20.

21 To him that overcometh [*overcomes wickedness and temptation through Christ's Atonement*] will I grant to sit with me in my throne [we *will be joint-heirs with Christ (Romans 8:17); exalted*], even as I also overcame, and am set down with my Father in his throne [*compare with D&C 76:107–8*].

22 He that hath an ear, let him hear what the Spirit saith unto the churches.

REVELATION 4

As mentioned previously, chapters 1–3 of Revelation deal mainly with John's day, especially chapters 2 and 3. Starting with this chapter, John will primarily be shown things that will take place in the future. Verse 1 specifically says that John will now be shown the future.

Among other things, he will be shown Heavenly Father seated on His throne of power and glory.

1 After this I [*John*] looked, and, behold, a door was opened in heaven: and the first voice [*the voice of the Savior; see 1:10–11*] which I heard was as it were of a trumpet [*a clear, definite sound whose source is unmistakable, and whose message is clear*] talking with me; which said, Come up hither, and I will shew [*pronounced "show"*] thee things which must be hereafter [*now we will talk about the future*].

JST Revelation 4:1

1 After this I looked, and behold, a door was opened into heaven; and the first voice which I heard was as it were of a trumpet talking with me; which said, Come up hither, and I will show thee things which must be hereafter.

Did you notice the first JST change to this verse? It changes "opened in heaven" to "opened into heaven," giving the sense that John was invited to look into heaven, where he will see the Father.

2 And immediately I was in the spirit: and, behold, a throne was set in heaven, and one [*Heavenly Father, see 5:7*] sat on the throne.

John now uses the highest

descriptive terms and superlatives such as precious jewel stones, and so forth, in attempting to describe the Father.

3 And he that sat [*upon the throne*] to look upon like a jasper and a sardine stone [*a very hard, deep orange-red jewel stone symbolic of something one would look upon with total awe and wonder*]: and there was a rainbow [*depicting glory and beauty*] round about the throne, in sight like unto an emerald.

JST Revelation 4:3

3 And he that sat there was to look upon like a jasper and a sardine stone; and there was a rainbow round about the throne, in sight like unto an emerald.

Abraham likewise described Heavenly Father as "sitting upon his throne, clothed with power and authority; with a crown of eternal light upon his head" (Abraham Facsimile 2, Fig. 3).

The JST changes for verse 4, next, are doctrinally very significant because they show that faithful Saints can become gods, rather than existing eternally as angels.

4 And round about the throne

were four and twenty seats: and upon the seats I saw four and twenty elders [*faithful elders from the seven "wards" mentioned in Revelation 1:11 who had died; see D&C 77:5*] sitting, clothed in white raiment [*white robes; Strong's, #2440; symbolic of exaltation*]; and they had on their heads crowns [*symbolic of authority and power; exaltation*] of gold [*gold represents the best; in other words, exaltation*].

JST Revelation 4:4

4 And in the midst of the throne [*symbolizing becoming "joint heirs" with God, rather than forever being "on-the-outside-looking-in" worshipers*] were four and twenty seats [*thrones; symbolic of royalty; in other words, exaltation—see Revelation 3:21*]; and upon the seats I saw four and twenty elders sitting, clothed in white raiment, and they had on their heads crowns like gold.

As indicated in the note in the JST verse above, Joseph Smith's inspired change to "in the midst of the throne" in place of "round about the throne" in the Bible is a vital doctrinal change. Most Christians are taught that the highest state of grace in the afterlife is to be in heaven, around the throne of

God, praising and worshiping Him forever. Perhaps that view has been derived in part from the translational error "round about the throne" found in verse 4 of the King James Version of the Bible as seen above.

The change to "in the midst of the throne" also correlates with Paul's teaching in Romans that we can become "joint heirs with Christ."

Romans 8:17

17 And if children, then heirs; heirs of God, and **joint-heirs with Christ**; if so be that we suffer with *him,* that we may be also glorified together.

Next, we see John's description of the power and glory of the Father couched in imagery understood by the Jews. It is based on the history of the Savior as Jehovah on Mt. Sinai as He gave the Ten Commandments. The mountain shook and there was thunder and lightning indicating His glory and power to the trembling children of Israel (Exodus 20:18).

5 And out of the throne proceeded lightnings and thunderings and voices: and there were seven lamps of fire [*the seven leaders of the seven "wards"*] burning [*shining*] before the throne [*in front of*

the throne of the Father], which are the seven Spirits of God.

JST Revelation 4:5

5 And out of the throne proceeded lightnings and thunderings and voices; and there were seven lamps of fire burning before the throne, which are the seven servants of God [*in other words, the presiding officers of the seven "wards" mentioned in Revelation 1:4*].

Among other things, the symbolism of the "seven lamps of fire" could mean that the seven presiding officers shine with light from the throne of God and radiate that light to the members of their "wards" and "branches." It is often said that our stake presidents and bishops bring light and instruction from God to us as members of their flocks.

Next, John will be shown the future of the earth as it eventually becomes a celestial planet.

6 And before [*in front of*] the throne there was a sea of glass [*the celestialized earth; see D&C 77:1, 130:9*] like unto crystal: and in the midst of the throne, and round about the throne, were four beasts [*see D&C 77:2–3*] full of eyes [*representing light and*

knowledge; D&C 77:4] before and behind [*in front and back*].

JST Revelation 4:6

6 And before the throne there was a sea of glass like unto crystal; and in the midst of the throne were the four and twenty elders; and round about the throne, were four beasts full of eyes before and behind.

Did you notice that an important portion of a phrase was left out of the Bible here? It was replaced in the JST verse, above, so that it now reads "and in the midst of the throne **were the four and twenty elders**." As a result, we learn from the Bible the doctrine that faithful people can become gods (see also D&C 76:58, 95; 132:20) and are symbolically represented as being "in the midst of the throne." They are thus "made equal with him" (D&C 88:107), whereas, animals do not become gods but can be "round about the throne" of God, praising Him.

As a reminder of the great value of the revelations given through Joseph Smith that help us understand the book of Revelation, let's take a moment and read an example that helps us understand the "sea of glass" mentioned in verse 6, above. In

Doctrine and Covenants, section 77, the Prophet answered questions about the book of Revelation.

D&C 77:1

1 Q. What is the sea of glass spoken of by John, 4th chapter, and 6th verse of the Revelation?

A. It is the earth, in its sanctified, immortal, and eternal state.

Elsewhere, Joseph Smith explained that this earth will serve as a Urim and Thummim to those who inherit celestial glory and dwell upon it.

D&C 130:9

9 This earth, in its sanctified and immortal state, will be made like unto crystal and will be a Urim and Thummim to the inhabitants who dwell thereon, whereby all things pertaining to an inferior kingdom, or all kingdoms of a lower order, will be manifest to those who dwell on it; and this earth will be Christ's.

Joseph Smith also said:

"When the earth was sanctified and became like a sea of glass, it would be one great urim and thummim, and the Saints could look in it and see as they are seen" (Smith, *HC*, 5:279).

We will get additional help from the Lord through Joseph Smith as we continue our study of Revelation.

By the way, many people wonder whether animals will be resurrected. The fact that John saw beasts in heaven around the throne of God is a simple answer to this question. You can also read in D&C 29:23–24 that all creatures will be resurrected.

Perhaps you have heard that animals will be able to talk in the next life. These verses of Revelation verify that that will be the case.

Continuing, John saw four beasts around the Father's throne (verse 6) and gave a brief description of each, next.

7 And the first beast was like a lion, and the second beast like a calf, and the third beast had a face as a man, and the fourth beast was like a flying eagle.

Joseph Smith gave additional detail for verses 6–7, above.

D&C 77:2–3

2 Q. What are we to understand by the four beasts, spoken of in the same verse?

A. They are figurative expressions, used by the Revelator, John, in describing heaven, the paradise of God, the happiness of man, and of beasts, and of creeping things, and of the fowls of the air; that which is spiritual being in the likeness of that which is temporal; and that which is temporal in the likeness of that which is spiritual; the spirit of man in the likeness of his person, as also the spirit of the beast, and every other creature which God has created.

3 Q. Are the four beasts limited to individual beasts, or do they represent classes or orders?

A. They are limited to four individual beasts, which were shown to John, to represent the glory of the classes of beings in their destined order or sphere of creation, in the enjoyment of their eternal felicity.

Next, John continues his description of the four beasts he saw in the vision.

8 And the four beasts had each of them six wings [*representing power to move, act, etc., in the service of God; D&C 77:4*] about him; and they were full of eyes within [*full of light and knowledge; D&C 77:4*]: and they

rest not day and night [*never stop being loyal to God*], saying, Holy, holy, holy [*in Hebrew culture, repeating something three times makes it the highest superlative; the very best*], Lord God Almighty [*Elohim*], which was, and is, and is to come [*in other words, He is eternal*].

9 And when those beasts give glory and honour and thanks to him [*the Father*] that sat on the throne, who liveth for ever and ever [*indicating that all created things respect and worship the Father*],

JST Revelation 4:9

9 And when those beasts give glory and honor and thanks to him that sits on the throne, who liveth forever and ever,

10 The four and twenty elders fall down before him that sat on the throne, and worship him that liveth for ever and ever [*these faithful elders are eternally loyal to God*], and cast their crowns before the throne [*showing humility, submission, and respect to the Father and His authority*], saying,

JST Revelation 4:10

10 The four and twenty elders fall down before him that sits

on the throne, and worship him that liveth forever and ever, and cast their crowns before the throne, saying,

11 Thou art worthy, O Lord, to receive glory [*praise; Strong's, #1391*] and honour and power: for thou hast created all things, and for thy pleasure [*according to Thy will; Strong's, #2307*] they are and were created.

REVELATION 5

Chapter 5 is the most complete description we have in the scriptures of the premortal council, often referred to as the "grand council," wherein Christ was chosen to be our Savior and Redeemer. It is significant to note that we were there in this council in heaven and cast our vote in favor of Christ when He was chosen to be our Redeemer. We read (**bold** added for emphasis):

"The contention in heaven was—Jesus said there would be certain souls that would not be saved; and the devil said he would save them all, and laid his plans before the grand council, **who gave their vote in favor of Jesus Christ.**" (Smith, *HC*, 6:314)

"At the first organization in

heaven we were all present and saw the Savior chosen and appointed, and the plan of salvation made and **we sanctioned it**." (Smith, *The Words of Joseph Smith*, p. 60)

According to the Bible, we rejoiced on this grand occasion:

Job 38:4–7

4 Where wast thou when I laid the foundations of the earth? declare, if thou hast understanding.

5 Who hath laid the measures thereof, if thou knowest? or who hath stretched the line upon it?

6 Whereupon are the foundations thereof fastened? or who laid the corner stone thereof;

7 When the morning stars sang together, and **all the sons of God shouted for joy**?

Most Christian religions do not believe in and, consequently, do not teach about a premortal life. If someone is willing to believe the Bible, this chapter of Revelation in conjunction with Job 38:4–7 and Jeremiah 1:5 presents a chance to help them understand that we did live before we came to earth.

This chapter also contains one of the greatest collections of significant symbolic words and phrases anywhere in the scriptures. You may find it helpful to become familiar with these. A partial list follows:

Symbolic Words and Phrases

Verse 1

right hand: covenant hand

him that sat on the throne: Heavenly Father (see verse 7)

a book: The Father's plan for us to be sent to this mortal world (Note that in Revelation 10:2, 8–10, "book" is a mission for John; see D&C 77:14; thus, "a book" can also be symbolical here of Christ's mission to be our Redeemer.)

written within and on the backside: a complete plan

sealed with seven seals: the 7,000 years of the earth's mortal existence (see D&C 77:7)

Verse 2

a strong angel: a mighty angel (we don't know who this is)

Who is worthy to open the book, and loose the seals thereof? Who can carry out the Father's plan for us?

Verse 3

neither to look thereon: No one could even come close to being our Savior and carrying out the Father's plan.

Verse 4

read the book: carry out the Father's plan for us

Verse 5

the Lion of the tribe of Juda: Christ (Jesus was from the tribe of Judah; see Hebrews 7:14)

the Root of David: Christ (see Revelation 22:16)

hath prevailed: can carry out the Father's plan

Verse 6

in the midst: the central focus

a Lamb: Christ; symbolic of being sacrificed

as it had been slain: The Atonement worked for us even in premortality, as if it had already been accomplished. (See Holland, "This Do in Remembrance of Me," *Ensign*, Nov. 1995, p. 67. See also *The Life and Teachings of Jesus and His Apostles*, Institute of Religion New Testament Student Manual, p. 336.)

seven horns (JST "twelve horns"): Horn symbolizes power. See scriptural examples in Topical Guide, page 218, under "horn."

seven (JST "twelve") Spirits of God sent forth into all the earth: Twelve Apostles

eyes: light and knowledge (see D&C 7:4)

Verse 7

he came and took the book: Jesus accepted the mission to be our Savior.

out of the right hand of him that sat upon the throne: Right hand often symbolizes covenants; Jesus covenanted with the Father.

We will now proceed with our study of chapter 5 as the vision given John the Revelator continues. In his account he recorded things he was shown regarding the great premortal council in heaven in which we all participated.

1 And I saw in the right hand [*the covenant-making hand*] of him [*the Father; 5:7*] that sat on the throne a book [*containing the Father's plan; can also symbolize a specific mission for our Elder Brother Jesus Christ*] written within [*on the inside*] and on the backside [*in*

other words, "complete," symbol-izing that the Father's plan for us is perfect and that the Atonement is perfect], sealed with seven seals *[containing information about the 7,000 years of the earth's temporal existence; see D&C 77:7]*.

JST Revelation 5:1

1 And I saw in the right hand of him that sits on the throne a book written within and on the back side, sealed with seven seals.

We use Revelation 10:2, 8–9, along with D&C 77:14 to show us that "book," as used in verse 1, above, is symbolic of a mission or calling.

2 And I saw a strong angel *[one high in authority]* proclaiming *[asking]* with a loud voice, Who is worthy to open the book, and to loose the seals thereof *[who can carry out the Father's plan of salvation, including the Atone-ment, for us]*?

JST Revelation 5:2

2 And I saw a strong angel, and heard him proclaiming with a loud voice, Who is worthy to open the book, and loose the seals thereof?

The lack of capable volunteers from among all of us in pre-mortality (except, of course,

the Firstborn spirit child of the Father), as described next in verse 3, is a dramatic reminder that "there shall be no other name given nor any other way nor means whereby salvation can come unto the children of men, only in and through the name of Christ" (Mosiah 3:17).

3 And no man *[no common man]* in heaven, nor in earth, neither under the earth, was able to open the book, neither to look thereon *[in other words, there was no one to carry out the Father's plan and perform the Atonement; this was a dramatic moment in the vision (a very effective teaching technique) which in John's mind created the need to know what happened next]*.

4 And I *[John]* wept much *[John has become deeply emotionally involved in the vision]*, because no man was found worthy to open and to read the book, neither to look thereon *[none of God's spirit children, except Jesus Christ, was even close to being worthy or able to carry out the Father's plan for us or perform the Atonement]*.

5 And one of the elders *[mentioned in Revelation 4:4]* saith unto me, Weep not: behold *[look!]*, the

Lion of the tribe of Juda [*Christ*], the Root of David [*Christ*], hath prevailed to open the book, and to loose the seven seals thereof. [*Jesus Christ can do it!*]

6 And I beheld [*I looked*], and, lo, in the midst of the throne and of the four beasts, and in the midst of the elders, stood a Lamb [*Christ*] as it had been slain [*symbolic of Christ's atoning blood, shed for us*], having seven horns and seven eyes, which are the seven Spirits of God sent forth into all the earth.

JST Revelation 5:6

6 And I beheld, and, lo, in the midst of the throne and of the four beasts, and in the midst of the elders, stood a Lamb as it had been slain, having twelve horns and twelve eyes, which are the twelve servants of God [*symbolic of the Twelve Apostles*], sent forth into all the earth.

Did you notice the change from "seven" to "twelve" in the JST? If you will refer back to the symbolism notes included at the beginning of Revelation in this study guide, you will note that the number 12 symbolizes God's divine organization here on earth.

7 And he [*Christ*] came and took the book [*accepted the calling*] out of the right hand [*covenant hand*] of him [*Elohim*] that sat upon the throne [*in other words, Jesus Christ made a covenant with the Father to be the Redeemer*].

Next, in verses 8–14, John beautifully describes all of heaven praising Christ for His willingness to perform the Atonement and be our Redeemer, thus carrying out the Father's plan.

8 And when he [*Christ*] had taken the book, the four beasts and four and twenty elders fell down before the Lamb, having every one of them harps [*in biblical culture, harps symbolize being in the presence of God*], and golden vials [*containers*] full of odours [*incense—see footnote 8a in your LDS English edition of the Bible; symbolic of prayers which rise up to God*], which are the prayers of saints.

The phrase "they sung a new song," in verse 9, next, is a scriptural phrase that means, in effect, that they could now rejoice over something that they could not rejoice about before. In other words, they can now sing praises to our Redeemer, whereas, they couldn't before, because He had not yet been chosen. Another example of "new song" can be found in D&C 84:98–102, where a new song can be sung about the Millennium, which has finally come at that point in that prophecy.

9 And they sung a new song, saying, Thou [*Christ*] art worthy to take the book [*see verse 1; in other words, the mission to be the Savior and work out the Father's plan*], and to open the seals thereof [*and to carry out the work planned for each of the 1,000-year periods of the earth's temporal history*]: for thou wast slain [*speaking of the Atonement as if it were already accomplished*], and hast redeemed us to God [*brought us back to the Father—see D&C 76:24*] by thy blood out of every kindred, and tongue, and people, and nation [*the gospel covenants are for all peoples of the world; the Pharisees of Jesus' day didn't like this concept because they felt that the Jews were superior to all other people and, consequently, all other people would be second class citizens in heaven*];

10 And hast made us unto our God kings and priests [*celestial exaltation; see Revelation 1:6; D&C 76:55–56*]: and we shall reign on the earth [*both during the Millennium (Revelation 20:4) and when it becomes the celestial kingdom; see D&C 132:20*].

11 And I beheld, and I heard the voice of many angels round about the throne [*of the Father; see Revelation 4:2 and 5:1*] and the beasts and the elders: and the number of them was ten thousand times ten thousand [*a hundred million*], and thousands of thousands [*plus millions more*];

The emphasis in verse 11, above, that there will be a great number of people in the celestial kingdom, is very comforting. You may wish to cross-reference verse 11 with Revelation 7:9, and also with D&C 76:67 in which we learn that there will be innumerable people in celestial glory. This is not surprising when we consider the missionary work that is being done in the spirit world as well as the fact that "all children who die before they arrive at the years of accountability are saved in the celestial kingdom of heaven." (See D&C 137:10.)

Along this same line, it is very encouraging to note that President Wilford Woodruff quoted D&C 137:7–9, referring to the fact that those who would have accepted the gospel here on earth if they had had a proper chance, will in the afterlife, and then said:

"So it will be with your fathers. There will be very few, if any, who will not accept the Gospel. . . . The fathers of this people will embrace the Gospel." (Woodruff, *Teachings of Presidents of the Church,* pp. 190–91)

12 Saying with a loud voice, Worthy is the Lamb [*Christ*] that was slain to receive power, and riches, and wisdom, and strength, and honour, and glory, and blessing.

13 And every creature which is in heaven [*birds, etc.*], and on the earth, and under the earth [*animals that burrow underground*], and such as are in the sea [*fish, etc.*], and all that are in them, heard I saying, Blessing [*praise*], and honour, and glory, and power, be unto him [*the Father*] that sitteth upon the throne, and unto the Lamb [*Christ*] for ever and ever [*all animals, birds, fish, etc., will be resurrected too as a result of Christ's Atonement; see D&C 29:23–24*].

14 And the four beasts said, Amen [*"We agree."*]. And the four and twenty elders fell down and worshipped him that liveth for ever and ever.

REVELATION 6

This is one of the most studied and well-known chapters in the book of Revelation. In it, the Lamb, Christ, opens six of the seven seals mentioned in Revelation 5:1. Joseph Smith tells us, in D&C 77:7, that each of the seals represents one thousand years of the earth's temporal or mortal existence. We understand this to mean that the earth has a total of 7,000 years from the time of the Fall of Adam and Eve to the end of the "little season" (D&C 88:111) at the end of the Millennium when the earth's temporal existence comes to an end. (See D&C 77:6.) It is important to remember that we do not know the exact date of Adam's Fall. (See Bible Dictionary under "Chronology" where it says, "Many dates cannot be fixed with certainty.") Thus, we cannot tell exactly where we are in relation to the 7,000 years.

In Revelation, chapter 6, we are given a brief overview of each of the first four-thousand-year periods of the earth's temporal existence, then a tiny bit more about the fifth thousand years, and yet a little more about the sixth-thousand-year period of the earth's mortal existence. In the chapters that follow, beginning with chapter 7, many more details will be given, which are to be fulfilled near the end of the sixth-thousand-year period and in the beginning of the seventh-thousand-year period, before the Savior's Second Coming. (See D&C 7:12–13.)

The fact that the Lamb, the Savior, opens the seals is symbolic of the fact that Christ is in charge of things here on earth, under the Father's direction, and is carrying out the Father's plan as shown in Revelation, chapter 5. (See notes for Revelation 5:1–4 and 5:5–7.)

Four "horsemen" are in this chapter, which are rather famous among Christians who study their Bibles, and which have given rise to many articles, books, movies, and discussions. With the aid of symbolism given in the introduction of Revelation in this study guide, we can see major insights and descriptions given for each of these one-thousand-year periods as summarized in the following chart:

Verses 1–2

The First Thousand Years

(ca. 4,000 to 3,000 BC):

"White" is symbolic of righteousness, purity, etc., and

"horse" is symbolic of victory, might, triumph, etc. Thus, there is a great triumph of righteousness during the first thousand years. We do not know who this horseman is, but two good possibilities would be Adam and Enoch.

Verses 3–4

The Second Thousand Years

(ca. 3,000 to 2,000 BC):

A red horse could symbolize the triumph of war, bloodshed, etc., possibly representing the wickedness during Noah's day. This horseman has a "great sword," representing terrible destruction.

Verses 5–6

The Third Thousand Years

(ca. 2,000 to 1,000 BC):

A black horse and its rider could symbolize evil, spiritual darkness, etc., as well as the blackness and depression that accompanies famine and wickedness. This period of the earth's history would include the days of Abraham, Joseph in Egypt, and the years of captivity in Egypt for the children of Israel.

Famine was a major aspect of life during this one-thousand-year period. Abraham's brother, Haran, starved to death during this period (see Abraham 2:1). In fact, the rider of the black horse is holding "a pair of balances in his hand," which can be symbolic of famine and can represent that every morsel of food must be carefully measured out during times of famine. (See Leviticus 26:26.) Additional famine symbolism is found in the phrases "A measure of wheat for a penny" and "three measures of barley for a penny." Here, a "penny" represents a day's wages (see Matthew 20:2) and a "measure of wheat" is about one quart. (See McConkie, *DNTC*, 3:480.)

Verses 7–8

The Fourth Thousand Years

(ca. 1,000 to 0 BC):

The fourth horse is pale and its rider is named Death. "Hell" seems to be following this horseman around and could symbolize that spirit prison is gaining many new inmates during this thousand-year period. The pale horse could represent that, after the riders of the red horse and the black horse have taken their toll, not much quality of life remains for those who have chosen wickedness as a lifestyle. It is during this time in history that we see Israel divided by civil war, Assyria carries the lost ten tribes away, Lehi and his family flee Jerusalem, the Babylonians conquer Jerusalem, Daniel is thrown into the lions' den, and the Romans become the rulers of the Holy Land.

The next two-thousand-year periods do not involve horsemen but do give a brief overview of events during those times.

Verses 9–11

The Fifth Thousand Years

(ca. AD 0 to 1,000):

The fifth seal would include the Savior's birth, the early Church, the persecutions of the Christians, and the beginning centuries of the dark ages. In verses nine through eleven, John was shown early martyrs, members of the Church organized by the Savior during His mortal mission who had been killed because they would not deny their testimonies. According to symbolism in verse 11, these righteous Saints were given white robes indicating that they had earned exaltation.

Verses 12–16

The Sixth Thousand Years

(ca. AD 1,000 to 2,000):

In these verses, John sees the Savior open the sixth seal and is shown some signs of the times, including a great earthquake (verse 12). Perhaps, as a result of this earthquake, "every mountain and island were moved out of their places." These and other signs of the times occurring in the sixth seal appear to make the wicked think that the end of the world has come. Whatever the case, events that occur in the sixth seal cause the wicked to wish for anything necessary to prevent them from facing God and answering to Him for their wickedness. These verses remind us that "wickedness never was happiness" (Alma 41:10), and that the wicked will be in great agony when faced with the evil and foolishness of their agency choices.

Remember also that we do not have an exact chronological date for the Fall of Adam and Eve. Therefore, the approximate dates for each of the six-thousand-year periods are exactly that—approximations.

Be aware also that D&C 77:12 and 13 inform us that Christ will not come at the end of the sixth-thousand-year period. Rather, a number of things will take place in the beginning of the seventh thousand years prior to His coming.

We will now study Revelation, chapter 6.

1 And I saw when the Lamb [*Christ*] opened one of the seals [*the first one, representing the first thousand years of the earth's temporal existence; i.e., approximately 4,000–3,000 BC (D&C 77:7)*], and I heard, as it were the noise of thunder, one of the four beasts saying, Come and see.

JST Revelation 6:1

1 And I saw when the Lamb opened one of the seals, one of the four beasts, and I heard, as it were, the noise of thunder, saying, Come and see.

2 And I [*John*] saw, and behold a white horse [*symbolically, white can mean righteousness and horse represents victory*]: and he that sat on him had a bow; and a crown [*authority*] was given unto him: and he went forth conquering, and to conquer [*one possible interpretation could be Adam. Another, Enoch and his victories with the City of Enoch*].

3 And when he [*Christ*] had opened the second seal [*3,000–2,000 BC*], I heard the second beast say, Come and see.

4 And there went out another horse that was red [*bloodshed, war*]: and power was given to him [*perhaps representing Satan and wicked, worldly leaders during the days of Noah*] that sat thereon to take peace from the earth, and that they should kill one another: and there was given unto him a great sword [*representing terrible destruction*].

5 And when he [*Christ*] had opened the third seal [*2,000–1,000 BC*], I heard the third beast say, Come and see. And I beheld [*I looked*], and lo a black horse [*evil, darkness, despair*]; and he that sat on him had a pair of balances [*representing famine; food had to be carefully measured and meted out*] in his hand.

> During this seal, Abraham went to Egypt because of famine. Later, Joseph was sold into Egypt. After he became prime minister under Pharaoh, his brothers came to him in Egypt because of famine. Also, the Israelites were held as slaves in Egypt during this period.

6 And I heard a voice in the midst of the four beasts say, A measure [*two U.S. pints*] of wheat for a penny [*a day's wages*], and three measures of barley for a penny; and see thou hurt not [*don't waste*] the oil and the wine [*terrible famine*].

JST Revelation 6:6

> 6 And I heard a voice in the midst of the four beasts say, A measure of wheat for a penny, and three measures of barley for a penny; and hurt not thou the oil and the wine.

7 And when he [*Christ*] had opened the fourth seal [*1,000–0 BC*], I heard the voice of the fourth beast say, Come and see.

> During this seal, we see the Assyrian captivity of the northern ten tribes of Israel and the ten tribes carried away about 722 BC and subsequently becoming the lost ten tribes; Babylonian captivity in about 588 BC; Daniel in the lions' den; and the Romans taking over prior to Christ's birth.

8 And I looked, and behold a pale horse [*not much left of Israel, few righteous people, terrible conditions among the wicked, etc.*]: and his name that sat on him was Death, and Hell followed with him. And power was given

unto them over the fourth part of the earth [*perhaps meaning not quite as severe destruction as in the windup scenes of the world depicted in Revelation 9:15*], to kill with sword [*military destruction*], and with hunger, and with death [*pestilence, plagues*], and with the beasts of the earth.

9 And when he [*Christ*] had opened the fifth seal [*AD 0–1,000*], I saw under the altar [*altar represents sacrifice*] the souls of them that were slain for the word of God [*for the gospel*], and for the testimony which they held [*those who gave their lives for the gospel's sake*]:

10 And they [*the people who had given their lives for the gospel*] cried with a loud voice, saying, How long, O Lord, holy and true, dost thou not judge and avenge our blood on them [*the wicked*] that dwell on the earth? [*When will the wicked get what is coming to them?*]

Joseph Smith asked this same basic question as he languished in Liberty Jail, as recorded in D&C 121. Habakkuk, an Old Testament prophet, likewise expressed the same concern (see Habakkuk 1), and the Lord answered him in Habakkuk 2:1–4.

11 And white robes [*symbolizing exaltation; 3:5*] were given unto every one of them [*the righteous martyrs in verse 9*]; and it was said unto them, that they should rest yet for a little season, until their fellowservants also and their brethren, that should be killed as they were, should be fulfilled [*in other words, others would have similar fates throughout earth's remaining history*].

12 And I beheld when he [*Christ*] had opened the sixth seal [*roughly AD 1,000–2,000*], and, lo, there was a great earthquake; and the sun became black as sackcloth of hair [*perhaps meaning black goat's hair used in weaving fabric*], and the moon became as blood [*great signs of the times in heaven and earth during this period of time*];

13 And the stars of heaven [*perhaps including satellites, airplanes, etc., in our day*] fell unto the earth, even as a fig tree casteth her untimely figs, when she is shaken of a mighty wind.

John now jumps ahead to the Second Coming for a few verses. Caution, do not put the Second Coming in the sixth seal. See headings to Revelation 8 and 9 in our LDS Bible and D&C 77:13.

14 And the heaven departed as a scroll when it is rolled together; and every mountain and island were moved out of their places [*one continent, one ocean again; D&C 133:22–24; Genesis 10:25*].

JST Revelation 6:14

14 And the heavens opened as a scroll is opened when it is rolled together; and every mountain, and island, was moved out of its place.

Next, we see the awful sense of accountability and fear that comes into the hearts and souls of the grossly wicked when they realize that they will now have to face the consequences of their intentional wickedness.

15 And the kings [*wicked political leaders*] of the earth, and the great men [*wicked and influential*], and the rich men, and the chief captains, and the mighty men, and every bondman, and every free man [*all the wicked*], hid themselves in the dens [*caves*] and in the rocks of the mountains [*like Isaiah said the wicked would do at the Second Coming; see Isaiah 2:19 and 2 Nephi 12, verses 10, 19, and 21*];

16 And said to the mountains and rocks, Fall on us, and hide us

from the face of him [*the Father; Revelation 5:1, 7, 13*] that sitteth on the throne, and from the wrath [*anger*] of the Lamb [*Christ*]:

17 For the great day of his [*the Savior's*] wrath is come; and who shall be able to stand [*who will be able to survive the Second Coming*]?

The answer to the question posed at the end of verse 17, above, is those living a terrestrial or celestial lifestyle. A quote verifies this answer. We read, "Because of the destruction of the wicked at the Savior's Second Coming, only righteous people will live on the earth at the beginning of the Millennium. They will be those who have lived virtuous and honest lives. These people will inherit either the terrestrial or celestial kingdom" (*Gospel Principles*, p. 263).

2 Nephi 12:10, 19, and 21; D&C 5:19; plus 76:81–85 and 88:100–101 tell us that those who live the wicked lifestyle of telestials (and, of course, sons of perdition), which includes lying, stealing, sexual immorality, and murder, will be destroyed by the Savior's glory at the Second Coming and will not be resurrected until after the Millennium is over.

REVELATION 7

John now returns to the sixth seal and tells us more about it. He will show us that great missionary work will take place during the sixth-thousand-year period of the earth's temporal existence. He will also show that many out of all nations will eventually attain exaltation. This chapter is perhaps best known for verse 4 in which the 144,000 are mentioned. We will say more about them when we come to that verse.

As we begin with verse 1, it helps to know that "wind," as used in the scriptures, is often symbolic of destruction. This symbolism is based on the dreaded "east wind" that sometimes blew in from the hot desert country east of Palestine and dried up and destroyed crops, often overnight.

1 And after these things I saw four angels [*with power and authority to save life or destroy, and to oversee the preaching of the gospel to the whole earth; D&C 77:8*] standing on the four corners of the earth [*symbolic of the whole earth*], holding the four winds [*north, east, south, and west winds, which symbolically have power to bless mankind from all directions or cause great*

destruction from all directions] of the earth, that the wind should not blow on the earth, nor on the sea, nor on any tree [*in other words, these four angels hold massive destruction back until the Restoration and ensuing gathering of the righteous have taken place; see verse 3*].

Joseph Smith taught that the four angels mentioned in verse 1, above, hold "power over the four quarters of the earth until the servants of God are sealed in their foreheads" (Smith, *TPJS*, p. 321).

President Wilford Woodruff taught that these four angels are already working to fulfill their prophesied role. He said, "Those angels have left the portals of heaven, and they stand over this people and this nation now, and are hovering over the earth waiting to pour out the judgments. And from this very day they shall be poured out" ("The Temple Worker's Excursion," *Young Women's Journal*, August 1894, p. 512).

2 And I saw another angel [*Elias; D&C 77:9; represents several angels with keys (see McConkie, DNTC, 3:492)*] ascending from the east ["*east" typically represents coming from heaven; an example of this symbolism is the*

sun, which symbolically represents celestial glory (1 Corinthians 15:40–41) and heaven, and,
of course, appears first from the
east], having the seal of the living
God: and he cried with a loud
voice to the four angels, to whom
it was given to hurt the earth and
the sea [they are not just destroying angels; they save life too,
D&C 77:8],

JST Revelation 7:2

2 And I saw another angel
ascending from the east, having
the seal of the living God; and I
heard him cry with a loud voice
to the four angels, to whom it
was given to hurt the earth and
the sea,

3 Saying, Hurt not the earth,
neither the sea, nor the trees [do
not allow the final destructions
prior to the Second Coming], till
we have sealed the servants of
our God [the righteous] in their
foreheads [i.e., the faithful and
those willing to be converted and
become faithful will be gathered
to the gospel before the final
destruction].

Concerning the sealing of "the
servants of our God in their
foreheads," mentioned in verse
3, above, it is helpful to know
that anciently some cultures

literally marked their foreheads
indicating which religion they
were loyal to.

Joseph Smith taught that the
sealing mentioned in verse 3,
above, "signifies sealing the
blessing upon their heads,
meaning the everlasting covenant, thereby making their calling and election sure" (Smith,
TPJS, p. 321).

4 And I heard the number of them
which were sealed: and there were
sealed an hundred and forty and
four thousand [these are not the
only ones saved; see verse 9] of
all the tribes of the children of
Israel.

JST Revelation 7:4

4 And the number of them who
were sealed, were an hundred
and forty and four thousand of
all the tribes of the children of
Israel.

Who are the 144,000? Joseph
Smith answered this question
for us in D&C 77:11. He said
they are high priests, 12,000
out of each of the tribes of
Israel, who will "bring as many
as will come to the church of
the Firstborn." The "church of
the Firstborn" is The Church
of Jesus Christ of Latter-day
Saints and often includes the
connotation of being exalted

(D&C 76:54–56). Thus, we see this great group of high priests much involved in the missionary work and gathering of the righteous spoken of in verses 1–3, above.

5 Of the tribe of Juda were sealed twelve thousand. Of the tribe of Reuben were sealed twelve thousand. Of the tribe of Gad were sealed twelve thousand.

6 Of the tribe of Aser were sealed twelve thousand. Of the tribe of Nepthalim were sealed twelve thousand. Of the tribe of Manasses were sealed twelve thousand.

7 Of the tribe of Simeon were sealed twelve thousand. Of the tribe of Levi were sealed twelve thousand. Of the tribe of Issachar were sealed twelve thousand.

8 Of the tribe of Zabulon were sealed twelve thousand. Of the tribe of Joseph were sealed twelve thousand. Of the tribe of Benjamin were sealed twelve thousand.

If you look carefully at verses 5–8 above, you will see that the tribes of Dan and Ephraim are missing. We have no idea why they are left out, and speculation does not help. We know for sure that they are not left out as far as the Lord's blessings are concerned, because many members of the Church, who are promised the "blessings of Abraham, Isaac, and Jacob (the blessings of exaltation—see Abraham 2:9–11) in their patriarchal blessings are from the lineage of Ephraim, and quite a number are from the tribe of Dan.

9 After this I beheld, and, lo, a great multitude, which no man could number [*in other words, many more than 144,000 are saved; see also D&C 76:67*], of all nations, and kindreds, and people, and tongues, stood before the throne [*of the Father*], and before the Lamb, clothed with white robes [*symbolic of celestial glory and exaltation*], and palms [*symbolic of joy and triumph, victory*] in their hands;

If you ever run into someone who wonders if it is true that only 144,000 will be saved (misinterpretation of verse 4), verse 9, above, provides wonderful evidence that such is not the case.

Next, we catch a glimpse of the great joy in the hearts of those who are saved as they praise the Father and Son for the salvation that has come to them through the Father's plan.

10 And cried with a loud voice, saying, Salvation to our God [*the Father*] which sitteth upon the throne, and unto the Lamb [*Christ*].

11 And all the angels stood round about the throne, and about the elders and the four beasts [*see notes in chapter 4*], and fell before the throne on their faces [*a way of showing humility and worship in biblical culture*], and worshipped God,

12 Saying, Amen ["*we agree*"]: Blessing, and glory, and wisdom, and thanksgiving, and honour, and power, and might, be unto our God for ever and ever. Amen.

John is now invited to become an active participant in the vision, as one of the elders asks him a question about what he has just seen. Notice his wise and careful answer.

13 And one of the elders answered [*asked a question*], saying unto me [*John*], What are these which are arrayed in white robes? and whence came they [*in other words, who are the people dressed in white mentioned in verse 9*]?

14 And I said unto him, Sir, thou knowest [*please tell me*]. And he said to me, These are they which came out of great tribulation [*trials and persecutions*], and have washed their robes [*had their sins cleansed by the Atonement of Christ; something each of us must do in our own lives; "washed their robes" is symbolic of repentance and obedience*], and made them white [*become clean*] in the blood of the Lamb [*the Atonement can cleanse us completely from our sins; compare with Isaiah 1:16–18*].

15 Therefore are they [*this is the reason they are*] before the throne of God [*they are in celestial glory*], and serve him day and night [*keep His commandments day and night*] in his temple [*another way of referring to the celestial kingdom—see Revelation 21:22*]: and he that sitteth on the throne shall dwell among them.

16 [*John now briefly and beautifully describes some benefits of celestial glory.*] They shall hunger no more, neither thirst any more; neither shall the sun light on them, nor any heat.

17 For the Lamb [*the Savior*] which is in the midst of the throne shall feed them, and shall lead them unto living fountains of waters: and God shall wipe away all tears from their eyes [*the final state of the righteous; in other words, it is worth*

repenting, being faithful, and re-
turning to God's presence!].

REVELATION 8

Many people think that the Savior's Second Coming will occur at
the end of the sixth seal. According to the Lord, this is not so. In
D&C 77:12, Joseph Smith tells
us that the things prophesied in
Revelation, chapter 8, will take
place "in the beginning of the
seventh thousand years," before
the coming of the Lord. Indeed,
we who live in the last days live in
a day when prophecies are being
fulfilled all around us. It is a glorious time to be alive, a time when
testimonies can be strengthened
by observing the fulfillment of
many ancient prophecies known
as the signs of the times, which
will lead up to the actual Second
Coming of the Lord. Let's watch
now and see some of the things
John the Beloved was shown that
will take place early in the seventh seal, before the Savior comes
to usher in the Millennium.

1 And when he [*Christ, Revelation 6:1*] had opened the seventh
seal [*roughly AD 2,000–3,000*],
there was silence in heaven about
the space of half an hour.

This "silence" is also mentioned
in D&C 88:95. We have not
been told yet what this means.
So far, in the opening of the
seals, we have been dealing
with the earth's time system.
Some people speculate about
this half hour of silence and
suggest that it might be about
21 years in the Lord's time
system, and thus we would have
21 years without revelation.
This has no merit, especially in
view of Daniel 2:35, 44–45, in
which we are assured that this
restored Church "shall stand
forever" and thus we will have
continuous revelation right up
to the Second Coming.

2 And I saw the seven angels which
stood before God; and to them were
given seven trumpets [*perhaps
symbolic of perfecting or finishing His work; in biblical number
symbolism, "seven" represents
being complete or perfection*].

The trumpets given to the seven
angels mentioned in verse 2,
above, could be symbolic of
preparations to announce specific events and circumstances
that will take place in the windup
scenes before the Second
Coming. For example, you
will see the first of the seven
angels sound his trumpet in
verse 7, below, announcing terrible plagues and pestilences,

designed, according to D&C 88:88–91, to get people's attention in the last days after they have basically rejected the humble testimony of missionaries.

We will pause to mention an interesting possibility in conjunction with biblical numerical symbolism and the number seven. As indicated in the symbolism notes provided at the beginning of this study guide, the number three represents God, and the number four represents man. Therefore, 3 (God) plus 4 (man) equals 7 (perfection), or in other words, when man works with God, the result is perfection, ultimately, exaltation.

3 And another angel came and stood at the altar [*worshipped*], having a golden censer [*symbolic of worship*]; and there was given unto him much incense [*incense rises, prayers "rise"; hence incense is symbolic of prayers; see 5:8*], that he should offer it with the prayers of all saints upon the golden altar which was before the throne [*in front of the throne of the Father; see Revelation 4:4 and 5:5; in other words, Saints and angels worship God*].

4 And the smoke of the incense, which came with the prayers of the saints, ascended up [*rose up*]

before God out of the angel's hand [*the prayers reached God*].

5 And the angel took the censer, and filled it with fire of the altar [*punishments from God*], and cast it into the earth [*punishments of God pour out upon the earth early in the seventh seal, before Second Coming*]: and there were voices, and thunderings, and lightnings, and an earthquake [*more signs of the times; compare with D&C 88:89–90*].

6 And the seven angels [*in verse 2, above*] which had the seven trumpets [*as mentioned in the note in verse 2, above, since "seven" is symbolic of completeness or perfection, this could be symbolic of the completing, perfecting, or finishing of all things necessary before the Second Coming; see D&C 77:12*] prepared themselves to sound.

Just a thought about verses 7–12, next. There is much use of symbolism. Symbolism can be understood many ways and thus can present many different messages to us as directed by the Holy Ghost. So it is with the symbolism in these next verses. One could easily look at the damage to earth, trees, grass, sea, rivers, fountains of waters, waters, sun, moon, and stars, as shown in this chapter, and consider it to be prophetic reference to severe ecological damage in the last days prior to the Second Coming.

Another possibility is that one could consider "trees" and "grass" to represent people, as is often the case in the scriptures. If so, the prophetic symbolism here could refer to damage done to people by evil in the last days. We could look at the "rivers," "fountains of waters," and "waters" and consider John 4:10 and 14 wherein the Savior teaches of the "living water" (the gospel, including the Atonement) and its cleansing and refreshing power in our lives. Then we could see prophetic reference to the damage done to the "living water" in people's lives by the wickedness in the last days. Again, we could look at the "sun, moon, and stars" as representing spiritual light from above and the darkening of them as spiritual darkness increases in the last days.

Chapter 8 also mentions hail, fire, blood, and so forth. It is interesting to observe that some of these plagues and pestilences to be poured out upon the earth in the last days, prior to the coming of the Lord, are reminiscent of some that took place in order to prepare the way for Moses and the children of Israel to gain freedom from Egyptian bondage. You will see that Revelation, chapter 16, contains a number of these plagues also. We will make a brief list of these plagues from both chapters 8 and 16, which lead us to realize that the ten plagues are, in effect, to be repeated in the last days before the Second Coming, and for the same purpose (to serve as a wake-up call to repent and be delivered from spiritual bondage). Thus, these plagues might be considered an example of "tough love" from a loving God as He strives to get the attention of and save more of His children.

From Revelation, chapter 8:

Verse 7: **hail and fire** (Exodus 9:23)

Verse 7: **blood** (Exodus 7:17)

Verse 8: **sun . . . darkened** (Exodus 10:21–22)

From Revelation, chapter 16:

Verse 2: **sores** (Exodus 9:9)

Verse 3: **blood** (Exodus 7:17)

Verse 8: **fire** (Exodus 9:23–24)

Verse 10: **darkness**
(Exodus 10:21–22)

Verse 13: **frogs** (Exodus 8:2)

Verse 21: **hail** (Exodus 9:18)

7 The first angel sounded, and there followed hail and fire mingled with blood [*similar to plagues in Egypt whose purpose likewise was to humble the wicked and prepare Israelites for redemption from wickedness*], and they were cast upon the earth: and the third part of trees was burnt up, and all green grass was burnt up [*perhaps indicating that significant amounts of earth's greenery will be destroyed prior to the Second Coming, rain forests razed, acid rain damage, etc.*].

8 And the second angel sounded, and as it were a great mountain burning with fire was cast into the sea: and the third part of the sea became blood [*similar to the plague in Egypt; Exodus 7:17*];

9 And the third part of the creatures which were in the sea, and had life, died; and the third part of the ships were destroyed [*much destruction everywhere*].

10 And the third angel sounded, and there fell a great star [*Lucifer; Isaiah 14:12 and D&C 76:25–27*] from heaven, burning as it were a lamp, and it fell upon the third part of the rivers, and upon the fountains of waters [*Satan provides counterfeit "living water," such as false religions and philosophies that cause terrible spiritual destruction*];

The true "living water" from Christ (John 4:10–14) brings soothing refreshment to the soul and eventual eternal life.

As John continues to relate what he saw in the vision, he tells us more about the devil and the destruction he causes in the lives of his followers in the last days.

11 And the name of the star is called Wormwood [*a very bitter substance; see Bible Dictionary under "Wormwood"; i.e., followers of Satan have a "bitter" fate*]: and the third part of the waters became wormwood; and many men died of the waters, because they were made bitter.

12 And the fourth angel sounded, and the third part of the sun was smitten, and the third part of the moon, and the third part of the stars; so as the third part of them was darkened [*perhaps symbolizing that there would be great spiritual darkness upon the earth in the last days before the coming of the Savior*], and the day

shone not for a third part of it, and the night likewise [*perhaps referring in part to spiritual darkness as well as physical darkness caused by burning oil fields, pollution, volcanic ash, etc., in the last days*].

JST Revelation 8:12

12 And the fourth angel sounded, and the third part of the sun was smitten, and the third part of the moon, and the third part of the stars; so that the third part of them was darkened, and the day shone not for a third part of it, and the night likewise.

The "one third" used in the above verses might be a symbolic tie-in with the one third who were cast out with Satan (Revelation 12:4), thus symbolizing their destructive influence upon the earth in the last days.

13 And I beheld, and heard an angel flying through the midst of heaven, saying with a loud voice, Woe, woe, woe, to the inhabiters [*inhabitants*] of the earth by reason of [*because of*] the other voices of the trumpet of the three angels [*in verse 2, above*], which are yet to sound [*i.e., worse is yet to come*]!

REVELATION 9

As you can see in the heading to Revelation, chapter 9, in your English version of the LDS Bible, this chapter continues with prophecies of events that will take place in the seventh seal, prior to the Second Coming. The Doctrine and Covenants confirms that they will occur "after the opening of the seventh seal, before the coming of Christ" (D&C 77:13).

The JST makes a very significant change to verse 1. As it stands in the Bible, it sounds like Lucifer is given the "key" to the bottomless pit. However, the JST informs us that the key is given to a powerful angel, through whose power and authority limits are placed upon Satan and his kingdom (see verse 4).

As John's vision continues, he informs us that the fifth angel (of the seven angels mentioned in chapter 8, verse 2) now blows his trumpet, announcing more plagues and devastations to take place in the last days before the Savior's coming.

1 And the fifth angel sounded, and I saw a star [*Lucifer*] fall from heaven unto the earth: and to him was given the key of the bottomless pit.

JST Revelation 9:1

1 And the fifth angel sounded, and I saw a star fall from heaven unto the earth; and to the angel was given the key of the bottomless pit.

In verses 2 and 3, next, we see all of the forces of hell unleashed in the final days before the coming of the Lord. There is much imagery here. We see "the bottomless pit" representing hell, Satan's kingdom, etc. We see smoke. In a house fire, smoke gets into everything and causes much damage. Thus, smoke, as used here, can be symbolic of evil and wickedness permeating every aspect of society. It arises out of the pit and darkens the light of the sun, reminding us that Satan's goal is to obscure the spiritual light that comes from above and leave us in spiritual darkness. Locusts bring to mind one of the plagues in Egypt (Exodus 10:4) and can symbolize seemingly countless hordes of the wicked working their evil designs upon the earth in the last days.

2 And he [*the angel in JST verse 1*] opened the bottomless pit [*allowed Satan to unleash all the forces of hell!*]; and there arose a smoke [*Satan's "dark" influence*] out of the pit, as the smoke of a great furnace; and the sun and the air were darkened by reason of the smoke of the pit. [*Satan and his evil hosts have great influence in the last days.*]

It might be frustrating to some that an angel with authority from God opens the bottomless pit and allows all the hellish forces of the devil to come forth in full array in the last days. Remember, though, that the Father's plan holds our agency in highest esteem, and this is a prophetic vision showing, among other things, that when mankind uses agency to choose evil and deepest, darkest wickedness, the powers of heaven draw back and allow those choices to wreak their bitter havoc.

3 And there came out of the smoke [*Satan's influence; see verse 2*] locusts [*symbolic of countless numbers of wicked in the last days*] upon the earth: and unto them was given power, as the scorpions of the earth have power [*scorpions have power to cause much suffering if people get close enough to them; so also is the case with wickedness*].

It is very important that we know that God has power over Satan and his wicked followers. He sets limits on them, as we see in verse 4, next.

4 And it was commanded them [*Satan and his hosts have limits put upon them by God*] that they should not hurt the grass of the earth, neither any green thing [*perhaps representing those who are still growing toward heaven*], neither any tree [*protection for the righteous; trees often represent people, for instance Isaiah 10:19*]; but only those men which have not the seal of God in their foreheads. [*Satan only has power to "hurt" the spirituality of the wicked who do not have God's seal, or in other words, are not loyal to God.*]

5 And to them [*Satan and his hosts*] it was given that they should not kill them [*the wicked in verse 4 who have not the seal of God in their foreheads*], but that they should be tormented five months [*through this torment it is hoped that some of them will see Satan for what he is and repent*]: and their torment was as the torment of a scorpion, when he striketh a man.

What is the significance of "five months" as seen in verse 5, above? Answer: We don't know. We do know that the life cycle of a locust (verse 3) is about five months (see Parry and Parry, *Understanding the Book of*

Revelation, p. 118), so it could symbolize that Satan and his evil forces have a limited time, as stated in Revelation 12:12. It could also be a symbolic tie-in with the "fifth angel" in verse 1.

6 And in those days [*the last days*] shall men seek death, and shall not find it; and shall desire to die, and death shall flee from them [*some plagues are worse than death*].

7 And the shapes of the locusts were like unto horses [*"horse" is symbolic of military victory; i.e., in John's vision of the future, Satan had much success with his armies of evil; almost countless people were involved in military actions in the last days*] prepared unto battle; and on their heads were as it were crowns like gold [*Satan's counterfeit rewards of power and wicked temporary glory lead many to follow him*], and their faces were as the faces of [*wicked*] men.

Did you notice that the "crowns" in verse 7, above, were "like" gold, or in other words, were not the real thing. Satan and his evil hosts are masters of counterfeiting, making evil look desirable, more attractive than the true "gold" (chapter 3, verse 18) that comes as the reward of righteousness and faithfulness to God.

8 And they had hair as the hair of women [*perhaps long hair might cause people in New Testament times to think of Samson's long hair and great strength and his destructive misuse of power; Judges 14–16*], and their teeth were as [*like*] the teeth of lions [*"lion" is symbolic of great power; i.e., they were able to inflict much damage, destruction*].

9 And they had breastplates [*armor*], as it were breastplates of iron; and the sound of their wings [*airplanes?*] was as the sound of chariots of many horses running to battle [*noises of modern military machinery in action?*].

10 And they had tails like unto scorpions [*modern warfare, tanks, flame throwers, rifles, etc.?*], and there were stings in their tails: and their power was to hurt men five months. [*We don't know for sure what the five months symbolize here or in verse 5. Perhaps it might simply be symmetry tying in with the fifth angel in verse one, thus meaning the "five months" or time spoken of by the fifth angel during which Satan rages in the last days.*]

11 And they had a king [*Satan*]

over them, which is the angel of the bottomless pit, whose name in the Hebrew tongue is Abaddon [*ruin, destruction; Strong's, #0003*], but in the Greek tongue hath his name Apollyon [*Destroyer; Strong's, #0623*].

Moses 5:24 gives another name for Satan. It is "Perdition," which means "utter loss" or "destruction." See also 2 Thessalonians 2:3.

12 One woe is past [*of the three woes spoken of in 8:13*]; and, behold, there come two woes more hereafter.

Just a bit more about the woes spoken of in verse 12, above. In chapter eight, verse 13, John was told that there were "three angels, which are yet to sound," in other words, three more "woes" or plagues to come. Revelation 9, verses 1–11, described one of the three "woes" for us, which leaves two more to come.

The second of the three "woes" mentioned in Revelation 8:13, and mentioned again in verse 12, above, begins with verse 13, next, and will be finished in Revelation 11:14 when John tells us that "the second woe is past."

13 And the sixth angel sounded

[*still dealing with occurrences in the beginning of the seventh seal, before the Lord comes; see heading to chapter 9 in our LDS English version of the Bible*], and I heard a voice from the four horns of the golden [*heavenly*] altar which is before God [*in other words, he heard a voice from heaven*],

The "four horns of the . . . altar," in verse 13, above, are symbolic, in biblical culture, of a place of safety, refuge, protection—see 1 Kings 1:50; in this case, it means heaven.

14 Saying to the sixth angel [*the sixth of the seven angels in Revelation 8:2*] which had the trumpet, Loose the four angels [*Satan's angels of destruction; counterfeits of God's four righteous angels in Revelation 7, a reminder that Satan is the great counterfeiter!*] which are bound [*by God's power*] in the great river Euphrates.

JST Revelation 9:14

14 Saying to the sixth angel which had the trumpet, Loose the four angels which are bound in the bottomless pit.

The JST, above, helps identify the four angels in verse 14 as being evil angels of destruction.

Did you notice that Joseph Smith deleted "the great river Euphrates" completely?

Apostle Bruce R. McConkie defined these angels. He said, "Four of Satan's mighty angels are loosed to influence and lead men in that final war which shall slay the third part of men" (McConkie, *DNTC*, 3:503).

15 And the four angels [*evil angels*] were loosed, which were prepared for an hour, and a day, and a month, and a year, for to slay the third part of men. [*Perhaps one-third ties in symbolically with the one third wicked in Revelation 12:4, indicating that Satan and his hosts will devastate a great number of people on earth, just as he did in the war in heaven.*]

We have not yet been told by authorized servants of the Lord what the "hour, and a day, and a month, and a year" means, in verse 15, above. But when the time comes, appointed by heaven, for these four evil angels of the devil to be released, they will gather great numbers of the wicked to fight against good, as described in verses 16–19, next.

16 And the number of the army of the horsemen [*Satan's wicked*]

followers] were two hundred thousand thousand [*200 million, or in other words, countless!*]: and I heard the number of them.

JST Revelation 9:16

16 And the number of the army of the horsemen were two hundred thousand thousand; and I saw the number of them.

17 And thus I saw the horses [*symbolic of military might and victory*] in the vision, and them that sat on them [*Satan and his followers*], having breastplates of fire, and of jacinth [*a precious stone, perhaps symbolizing that materialism will lead many to follow Satan; could also mean that misuse of wealth will cause much sorrow and destruction in the last days*], and brimstone [*molten sulphur; symbolic of destruction*]: and the heads of the horses were as the heads of lions [*capable of much destruction*]; and out of their mouths issued fire and smoke and brimstone [*terrible devastations will occur in the last days*].

18 By these three [*fire, smoke, and brimstone in verse 17, above*] was the third part of men killed, by the fire, and by the smoke, and by the brimstone, which issued out of their mouths.

19 For their power is in their mouth [*perhaps including, symbolically, the power of the media in the last days to destroy spirituality and goodness*], and in their tails [*perhaps referring to "scorpion" in verse 5, which could symbolize military weapons, tanks, flame throwers, missiles, etc.*]: for their tails were like unto serpents, and had heads, and with them they do hurt.

In many cases throughout the scriptural history of the world, such terrible destructions as John saw here in the vision have caused the remaining people to humble themselves and repent. But, according to this prophetic vision, in the last days leading up to the Second Coming, the wicked will not repent and things will continue to get worse.

20 And the rest of the men which were not killed by these plagues yet repented not [*a sad fact*] of the works of their hands, that they should not worship devils, and idols of gold, and silver, and brass, and stone, and of wood: which neither can see, nor hear, nor walk [*the remaining wicked went right on with their wicked lifestyles in spite of the destruction all around them*]:

21 Neither repented they of their

murders, nor of their sorceries [*witchcraft, etc.*], nor of their fornication [*sexual immorality*], nor of their thefts.

The sad prophetic fact given in verses 20–21, above, is also clearly taught in modern revelation:

D&C 84:96–98

96 For I, the Almighty, have laid my hands upon the nations, to scourge them for their wickedness.

97 And plagues shall go forth, and they shall not be taken from the earth until I have completed my work, which shall be cut short in righteousness—

98 Until all shall know me, who remain, even from the least unto the greatest, and shall be filled with the knowledge of the Lord, and shall see eye to eye [*during the Millennium*].

REVELATION 10

This chapter is particularly touching when one realizes that by this time (approximately AD 95), John has long been the only Apostle remaining from the Church that Jesus established in the Holy Land. He was told that he would "tarry" (see John 21:21–23 and D&C 7:3), but, as far as we know, nothing had yet transpired with respect to that promise. If that is the case, he is now an old man, likely in his nineties, and still banished on the Isle of Patmos. Imagine his feelings when he is told that he will yet prophesy before the nations and carry out a great mission among the people of the earth [verse 11]!

We know that he was indeed translated and has not yet died, rather, has continued assisting with the work of the Lord here on earth. He will continue to do so until the Second Coming (D&C 7:3), at which time he will be resurrected. As a translated being, we understand that he has similar privileges and blessings to those of the Three Nephites, including being able to pray and be transported wherever he needs to be to appear to people and minister to them (3 Nephi 28:30). You can read more about the Three Nephites in 3 Nephi 28.

Before John accepts the calling and mission to continue living on earth as a translated being and continuing with the work of the Lord in saving souls, he will be shown some of the very final prophetic scenes before the Millennium begins (verses 1–6).

1 And I saw another mighty angel [*this appears to be the seventh of the angels in 8:2; if so, it might be Adam, the "seventh angel" in D&C 88:106, 110, 112*] come down from heaven, clothed with a cloud: and a rainbow was upon his head, and his face was as it were the sun, and his feet as pillars of fire [*quite a description of Michael or Adam, if he is indeed the seventh angel spoken of here*]:

> The "rainbow upon his head" in verse 1, above, could tie in with the "rainbow round about the throne" of the Father, in Revelation 4:3. If so, it might be symbolic of the splendid power of God and of exaltation.

2 And he had in his hand a little book [*a mission for John; see verses 8–10, also D&C 77:14*] open: and he set his right foot upon the sea, and his left foot on the earth [*D&C 88:110; in other words, this angel has a large jurisdiction*],

3 And cried with a loud voice, as when a lion roareth: and when he had cried, seven thunders uttered their voices [*seven angels with seven seals; D&C 88:108–10*].

> Elder Bruce R. McConkie said, "It appears from the added and clarifying knowledge revealed to Joseph Smith that the seven thunders which here utter their voices are the seven angels reciting in some detail that which is to be in each of the thousand-year periods of the earth's temporal continuance" (McConkie, *DNTC*, 3:505).

Elder McConkie also gave another possible interpretation. He said, "It also appears that John's vision prefigured what is to be when the events occur and that the promised proclamations shall yet be made when the hour for Millennial peace actually arrives" (Ibid.). Brother McConkie then quoted D&C 88:108–10.

D&C 88:108–10

108 And then shall the first angel again sound his trump in the ears of all living, and reveal the secret acts of men, and the mighty works of God in the first thousand years.

109 And then shall the second angel sound his trump, and reveal the secret acts of men, and the thoughts and intents of their hearts, and the mighty works of God in the second thousand years—

110 And so on, until the seventh angel shall sound his trump; and he shall stand forth upon

the land and upon the sea, and swear in the name of him who sitteth upon the throne, that there shall be time no longer; and Satan shall be bound, that old serpent, who is called the devil, and shall not be loosed for the space of a thousand years.

4 And when the seven thunders had uttered their voices, I [*John*] was about to write: and I heard a voice from heaven saying unto me, Seal up those things which the seven thunders uttered, and write them not [*in other words, they are not yet to be revealed to the world in the scriptures*].

JST Revelation 10:4

4 And when the seven thunders had uttered their voices, I was about to write; and I heard a voice from heaven saying unto me, Those things are sealed up which the seven thunders uttered, and write them not.

5 And the angel [*in verses 1 and 2, above*] which I saw stand upon the sea and upon the earth lifted up his hand to heaven,

6 And sware [*promised*] by him that liveth for ever and ever [*spoke with authority from God*], who created heaven, and the things that therein are, and the earth, and the things that therein are, and the sea, and the things which are therein, that there should be time no longer [*that there will be no more delay; in other words, "Let the Millennium begin"*]:

The phrase "there should be time no longer," as found in verse 6, above, also implies the end (for a thousand years) of the time of wickedness and persecution (because Satan will be bound for a thousand years as stated in D&C 88:110, quoted above). It also indicates that the "time" of waiting for justice to fall upon the wicked, as enquired about by the faithful martyrs in Revelation 6:9–10, is over.

7 But in the days of the voice of the seventh angel, when he shall begin to sound, the mystery [*plans; Strong's, #3466*] of God should be finished [*completed; Strong's, #5055*], as he hath declared to his servants the prophets.

Next, in verses 8–11, we see John accept his mission to remain on earth until the Second Coming and serve as a translated being.

8 And the voice which I heard from heaven spake unto me again, and said, Go and take the

little book [*mentioned in verse 2, above; a mission for John; D&C 77:14*] which is open in the hand of the angel which standeth upon the sea and upon the earth.

9 And I went unto the angel, and said unto him, Give me the little book [*I accept the mission*]. And he said unto me, Take it, and eat it up [*"internalize" it, make it a part of you*]; and it shall make thy belly bitter, but it shall be in thy mouth sweet as honey [*being a servant of God to the people has both bitter and sweet aspects*].

10 And I took the little book out of the angel's hand, and ate it up [*"internalized it"; made it a part of me*]; and it was in my mouth sweet as honey: and as soon as I had eaten it, my belly was bitter [*working with stubborn, unrepentant people can indeed cause indigestion!*].

11 And he said unto me, Thou must prophesy again before many peoples, and nations, and tongues, and kings. [*In other words, you have a great mission yet to perform on earth, a very significant and encouraging statement, since John at this time, about AD 95, was banished on the Isle of Patmos.*]

As mentioned in the introduction to this chapter, above, in D&C 7, we are told that John will "tarry" or remain until the Second Coming. In June 1831, Joseph Smith said "that John the Revelator was then among the ten tribes of Israel . . . to prepare them for their return" (Smith, *HC*, 1:176).

REVELATION 11

We are not alone in the Christian world in believing that the events of the last days spoken of in this chapter will take place. This chapter is one of the best known among Christians throughout the world. They, like we, believe that the mission of these two witnesses (verse 3), ending with their martyrdom and being brought back to life, will signify that the Second Coming of the Savior is close. Revelation 11:3 refers to them as "two witnesses," and Revelation 11:10 refers to them as "two prophets." In D&C 77:15, the Prophet Joseph Smith calls them "two prophets." Therefore, we see them as two witnesses, fulfilling the law of witnesses (D&C 6:28) and as two prophets holding the keys to control the elements, and so forth, as shown in verse 6.

In fact, since the First Presidency

and the Quorum of the Twelve Apostles are all "prophets, seers, and revelators," we see the two prophets spoken of here in Revelation as being two of the First Presidency and Quorum of the Twelve who are serving at the time of the fulfillment of this prophecy.

It is interesting to point out several parallels between the ministry of these two prophets and the ministry of the Savior. For instance, Christ's formal mission was carried out in the Holy Land and lasted about three years. The mission of these two prophets in the last days will be to the Holy Land and will last about three years. The Savior is the "light of the world." The two prophets are "candlesticks" (verse 4), which carry the light from the Savior to the world. Jesus demonstrated His power over the elements during His mortal ministry. The two prophets will be given power over the elements during their ministry (verse 6). Christ was crucified when He had completed His mortal mission. The two prophets will be killed after they have completed their mission (verse 7). The wicked rejoiced in the Savior's death. The wicked will rejoice in the slaying of the two prophets (verses 8–10).

Jesus was resurrected after three days. The two will be resurrected (see heading to chapter 11 in your LDS English version of the Bible) after three and a half days. Great destruction accompanied the death of the Savior. Great destruction will accompany the resurrection of the two prophets (verse 13). Many were converted by Christ's resurrection. Many will be converted after the resurrection of these two prophets (verse 13, last phrase).

1 [*John is the only living apostle remaining in the eastern hemisphere at this time (Jesus had called twelve disciples to serve among the Nephites on the western hemisphere—see 3 Nephi 12:1; 19:4). In the vision, he is told here to see how the Church is doing in his day.*] And there was given me [*John*] a reed [*a measuring device*] like unto a rod: and the angel stood, saying, Rise, and measure the temple of God, and the altar, and them that worship therein [*in other words, study current conditions among the Saints; see how they "measure up"*].

2 But the court [*the courtyard or temple grounds*] which is without [*outside of*] the temple leave out, and measure it not; for it is

given unto the Gentiles [*apostasy is coming*]: and the holy city [*Jerusalem*] shall they tread under foot forty and two months. [*This is perhaps referring to the 42 months spoken of in verse 3 since Jerusalem will be downtrodden by Gentiles for hundreds of years. The universal apostasy alluded to here will end in the spring of 1820 when Joseph Smith has his first vision.*]

Next, John is shown more of the future when he sees in the vision two mighty prophets who will minister to the Jews in the last days before the Second Coming and then will be killed and left lying in the streets of Jerusalem while wicked people throughout the world rejoice at their death.

3 And I will give power unto my two witnesses [*two prophets "to the Jewish nation in the last days"; D&C 77:15*], and they shall prophesy [*serve, minister, prophesy, teach, etc.*] a thousand two hundred and threescore days [*42 months or 3 1/2 years, about the same length as Christ's ministry*], clothed in sackcloth [*in humility*].

4 These are the two olive trees [*olive trees provide olive oil for lamps so people can be prepared to meet Christ; compare with the parable of the ten virgins in Matthew 25:1–13*], and the two candlesticks [*hold light so people can see clearly*] standing before the God of the earth [*who represent God to the people*].

5 And if any man will hurt them [*the two prophets*], fire [*the power of God to destroy*] proceedeth out of their mouth, and devoureth their enemies [*the two prophets will be protected during their mission*]: and if any man will hurt them, he must in this manner be killed [*he will be killed by the power of God; Strong's, #1163*].

6 These [*two prophets*] have power to shut heaven [*have the power of God; compare with the prophet Nephi in Helaman 10:5–10 and 11:1–6*], that it rain not in the days of their prophecy: and have power over waters to turn them to blood, and to smite the earth with all plagues [*to encourage people to repent; to deliver from evil, bondage, as with the plagues in Egypt*], as often as they will.

7 And when they shall have finished their testimony [*ministry*], the beast [*Satan*] that ascendeth out of the bottomless pit [*Revelation 9:1–2*] shall make war against them [*the two prophets*], and shall overcome them, and kill them.

Have you noticed that there is no scriptural evidence that Satan himself can actually kill mortal people? He must incite his mortal followers to do it for him.

8 And their dead bodies shall lie in the street of the great city [*Jerusalem*], which spiritually is called Sodom and Egypt [*extremely wicked, through and through*], where also our Lord was crucified.

It appears likely from verse 9, next, that technology and mass media will play a significant role in reporting the death of these two prophets to the entire world. It is interesting to note, if our thinking is correct, that the reporters and media controllers will be so pleased that the prophets are dead that they will continue full coverage of the event for three and a half days, at which time the "party" will be over as the two prophets are resurrected and taken up—verses 11–12.

9 And they [*the wicked*] of the people and kindreds and tongues and nations shall see their dead bodies three days and an half [*perhaps symbolically tying in with their three-and-a-half-year ministry, as well as the Savior's three days in the tomb; the Savior was killed, too, by the wicked for trying to save them*], and shall not suffer [*allow*] their dead bodies to be put in graves. [*Many in eastern cultures consider it to be the ultimate insult not to bury a person's dead body; also, many believe that if the body is not buried, the spirit is bound to wander the earth in misery forever.*]

10 And they that dwell upon the earth [*not just people in Jerusalem; implies that knowledge of the death of the two prophets will be known worldwide*] shall rejoice over them, and make merry, and shall send gifts one to another [*people all over the world will cheer and send gifts to one another to celebrate the deaths of these two prophets*]; because these two prophets tormented them [*the wicked*] that dwelt on the earth [*implies that these prophets' influence was felt and irritated the wicked far beyond Jerusalem*].

11 And after three days and an half the Spirit of life from God entered into them [*they are resurrected at this time; see heading to chapter 11 in your LDS English version of the Bible; also see McConkie, DNTC, 3:511*], and they stood upon their feet; and

great fear fell upon them which saw them.

12 And they [*the wicked who were celebrating*] heard a great voice from heaven saying unto them [*the two slain prophets*], Come up hither. And they ascended up to heaven in a cloud; and their enemies beheld [*saw*] them.

13 And the same hour [*immediately*] was there a great earthquake, and the tenth part of the city fell, and in the earthquake were slain of men seven thousand: and the remnant were affrighted, and gave glory to the God of heaven [*perhaps implying that some of the wicked were converted as was the case at the time of the Savior's crucifixion and resurrection and also when Lazarus was brought back from the dead; if so, the deaths of the two prophets bore immediate fruit in helping some begin returning to God*].

14 The second woe [*Revelation 9:12–21; 10; 11:1–13*] is past [*one more to go; Revelation 8:13*]; and, behold, the third woe [*the burning at the Second Coming*] cometh quickly.

15 And the seventh angel sounded; and there were great voices in heaven, saying, The kingdoms of this world are become the kingdoms of our Lord, and of his Christ [*Christ will now come to rule and the Millennium will begin*]; and he shall reign for ever and ever.

JST Revelation 11:15

15 And the seventh angel sounded; and there were great voices in heaven, saying, The kingdoms of this world are become the kingdom of our Lord, and of his Christ; and he shall reign for ever and ever.

Even though the JST change for verse 15, above, consisted only of changing "kingdoms" to "kingdom," the change is doctrinally significant. When the Savior comes to rule and reign on earth for the thousand years, He will have just one kingdom on earth. It will be a theocracy with Him as "Lord of lords, and King of kings" (Revelation 17:14) and it will be a time of unity and peace.

16 And the four and twenty elders [*who asked how long they must wait for justice to be done upon the wicked; Revelation 6:10*], which sat before God on their seats, fell upon their faces [*a show of humility and respect in Bible culture*], and worshipped God,

17 Saying, We give thee thanks,

O Lord God Almighty, which art, and wast, and art to come [*in other words, the Lord is eternal*]; because thou hast taken to thee thy great power [*You have finally come and taken over*], and hast reigned [*during the Millennium will finally rule the earth*].

The commentary and witness of the twenty-four elders (verse 16) in the vision continues as they explain what happens to the wicked and the righteous at the time of the Savior's coming.

18 And the nations were angry, and thy wrath [*righteous anger at the wicked*] is come, and the time of the dead, that they should be judged, and that thou shouldest give reward unto thy servants the prophets, and to the saints, and them that fear [*respect and honor*] thy name, small and great [*the hardly known righteous as well as the widely-known righteous*]; and shouldest destroy them [*the wicked*] which destroy [*corrupt*] the earth.

It helps with verse 19, next, to understand that the ark of the covenant was behind the veil in the Holy of Holies in Israel's temple, and when the high priest passed through the veil into the presence of the ark, it symbolized entering into the presence of God; thus, the symbolism here is that the righteous may now enter into the presence of the Lord as He comes to earth to rule and reign for a thousand years.

19 And the temple of God was opened in heaven, and there was seen in his temple the ark of his testament [*the ark of the covenant*]: and there were lightnings, and voices, and thunderings, and an earthquake, and great hail [*perhaps this last phrase is a brief review of woes and events leading up to the Second Coming as mentioned in verses 13 and 15, above, as well as elsewhere, rather than being a prophecy of things yet to come*].

REVELATION 12

The Prophet Joseph Smith revised this chapter of Revelation more than any other in the JST. He changed the verse sequence in several places. For your convenience, the entire Joseph Smith Translation of Revelation, chapter 12, has been included at the end of this chapter. You may wish to read it through entirely before coming back and continuing your study with verse 1, next.

As John continues to relate what he saw in the vision, we see that Satan has attempted, from very early on (including premortality), to stop the establishment of the true gospel of Jesus Christ among our Father's children.

1 And there appeared a great wonder in heaven; a woman [*the true Church—see JST, verse 7*] clothed with the sun, and the moon under her feet [*symbolic of beauty and glory*], and upon her head a crown [*symbolic of power to bring exaltation to true followers of Christ*] of twelve stars [*the twelve Apostles*]:

JST Revelation 12:1

1 And there appeared a great sign in heaven, in the likeness of things on the earth; a woman clothed with the sun, and the moon under her feet, and upon her head a crown of twelve stars.

Next, we see that the role of the Church is to establish the kingdom of God on the earth.

2 And she [*the Church*] being with child [*the kingdom of God—see JST 12:7*] cried, travailing in birth and pained to be delivered [*labor pains; symbolic of the fact that there are labor and pain involved in bringing forth the kingdom of God*].

JST Revelation 12:2

2 And the woman being with child, cried, travailing in birth, and pained to be delivered.

In verses 3 and 4, next, John saw Lucifer among us in premortality as "an angel of God who was in authority in the presence of God" (D&C 76:25) who had great power and attracted one-third of our Father's children to become his loyal followers in his rebellion.

3 And there appeared another wonder [*"another sign," see JST verse 4, below*] in heaven; and behold a great red dragon [*Lucifer; see verse 9*], having seven heads and ten horns, and seven crowns upon his heads [*representing the fact that Satan has great power, has many "front" organizations behind which he attempts to camouflage himself as he strives to defeat the Father's plan*].

Verse 4, next, shows us that Satan strives to stop the establishment of the Church in its earliest stages. This can apply to the restorations of the gospel throughout the history of the earth as well as the beginnings of testimony and conversion in the lives of individuals.

4 And his tail drew the third part of the stars of heaven [*one-third followed Satan in the war in heaven; D&C 29:36*], and did cast them to the earth [*the spirits who followed Lucifer are here on earth!*]: and the dragon [*Satan*] stood before the woman [*the Church*] which was ready to be delivered [*ready to bring forth the kingdom of God*], for to devour her child [*the kingdom of God*] as soon as it was born [*started*].

The JST combines verses 3 and 4, above.

JST Revelation 12:4

4 And there appeared another sign in heaven; and behold, a great red dragon, having seven heads and ten horns, and seven crowns upon his heads. And his tail drew the third part of the stars of heaven, and did cast them to the earth. And the dragon stood before the woman which was delivered, ready to devour her child after it was born.

5 And she [*the Church; JST 12:3, 7*] brought forth a man child [*the kingdom of God and His Christ; JST 12:7*], who was to rule all nations with a rod of iron [*during the Millennium (which John has just seen in the vision; see Revelation 11:15–19) the kingdom of God will be established and the iron rod, the word of God, will be in full effect*]: and her child was caught up unto God, and to his throne.

JST Revelation 12:3

3 And she brought forth a man child, who was to rule all nations with a rod of iron; and her child was caught up unto God and his throne.

Next, John sees the Great Apostasy that took place after the Savior was crucified and His Apostles martyred.

6 And the woman fled into the wilderness [*symbolic of the Great Apostasy, when the Church was gone for many centuries*], where she hath a place prepared of God, that they should feed her there a thousand two hundred and three-score days.

JST Revelation 12:5

5 And the woman fled into the wilderness, where she had a place prepared of God, that they should feed her there a thousand two hundred and threescore years.

Did you notice that the JST changes "days" to "years" at the end of the verse?

Next, John refers back to the

war in heaven. This is a good example of the fact that the ancient prophets, including John and Isaiah, were not concerned about keeping accounts in straight chronological order. This can be confusing to us today who tend to like things kept in chronological order.

7 And there was war in heaven [*a war of opinions, words, truth, error, light, darkness, and so forth, which continues here on earth today*]: Michael [*Adam*] and his angels [*righteous spirits*] fought against the dragon [*Satan*]; and the dragon fought and his angels [*the evil spirits who followed Satan*],

As you can see, here the JST versification is not the same as in Revelation in the Bible. This is because Joseph Smith combined verses 3 and 4 in the JST.

JST Revelation 12:6

6 And there was war in heaven; Michael and his angels fought against the dragon; and the dragon and his angels fought against Michael;

The JST adds much to verse 8, next.

8 And prevailed not; neither was their [*Satan and his followers*]

place found any more in heaven.

JST Revelation 12:7

7 And the dragon prevailed not against Michael, neither the child, nor the woman which was the church of God, who had been delivered of her pains, and brought forth the kingdom of our God and his Christ.

9 And the great dragon was cast out, that old serpent, called the Devil, and Satan, which deceiveth the whole world: he was cast out into the earth, and his angels were cast out with him.

JST Revelation 12:8

8 Neither was there place found in heaven for the great dragon, who was cast out; that old serpent called the devil, and also called Satan, which deceiveth the whole world; he was cast out into the earth; and his angels were cast out with him.

Verse 9 (JST, verse 8), above, is one of the places in scripture where we find the doctrine that the wicked premortal spirits who followed the devil in the war in heaven are now on earth where they can tempt and strive to lead us astray.

10 And I heard a loud voice saying in heaven, Now is come salvation

[*in other words, now people will be able to go down to earth and live and choose between good and evil, and thus earn salvation; see 2 Nephi 2:11*], and strength, and the kingdom of our God, and the power of his Christ: for the accuser [*Satan*] of our brethren is cast down, which accused them before our God day and night.

The JST breaks verse 10, above, into two verses.

JST Revelation 12:9–10

9 And I heard a loud voice saying in heaven, Now is come salvation, and strength, and the kingdom of our God, and the power of his Christ;

10 For the accuser of our brethren is cast down, which accused them before our God day and night.

One of Satan's effective tools of destruction is mentioned in verse 9 (JST, verse 10), above. It is that of attempting to discredit them by accusing righteous people, including Church leaders, of having impure motives as they strive to teach and preach the gospel.

An encouraging and vital doctrine is seen in verse 11, next. It is that the righteous can and will overcome Satan through the Atonement of Jesus Christ.

11 And they [*the righteous*] overcame him [*Satan and his evil*] by the blood of the Lamb [*through the Atonement of Christ*], and by the word of their testimony [*they kept their covenants*]; and they loved not their lives unto the death [*they were willing to give all to gain exaltation*].

12 Therefore rejoice, ye heavens, and ye that dwell in them. Woe to the inhabiters of the earth [*there will be trouble because Satan is here and you will have to choose right from wrong under severe pressure*] and of the sea! for the devil is come down unto you, having great wrath [*Satan is really "turning up the pressure"*], because he knoweth that he hath but a short time.

The JST rearranges verses 11–12, above, as follows:

JST Revelation 12:11–12

11 For they have overcome him by the blood of the Lamb, and by the word of their testimony; for they loved not their own lives, but kept the testimony even unto death. Therefore, rejoice O heavens, and ye that dwell in them.

12 And after these things I

heard another voice saying, Woe to the inhabiters of the earth, yea, and they who dwell upon the islands of the sea! for the devil is come down unto you, having great wrath, because he knoweth that he hath but a short time.

13 And when the dragon saw that he was cast unto the earth, he persecuted the woman [*the Church; this is the time of Satan's power*] which brought forth the man child [*the kingdom of God*].

JST Revelation 12:13

13 For when the dragon saw that he was cast unto the earth, he persecuted the woman which brought forth the man child.

John now returns to the Great Apostasy, mentioned in verse 6, above, to give us more details about it.

14 And to the woman were given two wings of a great eagle, that she might fly into the wilderness [*universal apostasy*], into her place, where she is nourished for a time, and times, and half a time [*we don't know what this means; one possibility could be 1 time plus 2 times plus 1/2 a time; i.e., 3 1/2 times, which might symbolically tie in with other uses of 3 1/2, such*

as in Revelation 11:3 where the Lord preserves the two prophets for three and a half years], from the face of the serpent [*Satan*].

JST Revelation 12:14

14 Therefore, to the woman were given two wings of a great eagle, that she might flee into the wilderness, into her place, where she is nourished for a time, and times, and half a time, from the face of the serpent.

15 And the serpent cast out of his mouth water as a flood after the woman [*symbolically, just as flood waters reach and get into everything in their path, so also Satan tries to get to us from every angle*], that he might cause her to be carried away of [*destroyed by*] the flood.

JST Revelation 12:15

15 And the serpent casteth out of his mouth water as a flood after the woman, that he might cause her to be carried away of the flood.

The water in verse 15, above, might remind us of the filthy water seen in Nephi's vision (1 Nephi 12:16).

16 And the earth helped the woman [*earth is designed and created to*

help us return to the Father; all things in it bear record of Him to us; Moses 6:63], and the earth opened her mouth, and swallowed up the flood which the dragon cast out of his mouth.

JST Revelation 12:16

16 And the earth helpeth the woman, and the earth openeth her mouth, and swalloweth up the flood which the dragon casteth out of his mouth.

17 And the dragon [Satan] was wroth [angry] with the woman [the Church], and went to make war with the remnant of her seed [the Saints in the last days], which keep the commandments of God, and have the testimony of Jesus Christ.

JST Revelation 12:17

17 Therefore, the dragon was wroth with the woman, and went to make war with the remnant of her seed, which keep the commandments of God, and have the testimony of Jesus Christ.

As mentioned at the beginning of this chapter, the complete JST of chapter 12 has been included here so you can read it in the order Joseph Smith arranged the verses. Notes for teaching purposes have also been included.

JST Revelation 12:1–17

1 And there appeared a great sign in heaven, in the likeness of things [symbolic of things] on the earth; a woman [the Church, see verse 7] clothed with the sun [symbolic of beauty, glory, and power to bring us to exaltation] and the moon under her feet, and upon her head a crown [symbolic of power, authority; exaltation] of twelve stars [the Twelve Apostles].

In this imagery, woman brings forth the greatest, highest good. In contrast, in Satan's work, see Revelation 17:1–6 and elsewhere, the woman, "the whore of all the earth" (1 Nephi 14:11), brings forth the greatest evil. Perhaps this is symbolic of the power of women, both for good and for evil.

2 And the woman being with child [verse 7, the kingdom of God and His Christ], cried, travailing in birth [labor pains], and pained to be delivered [it requires much pain and effort to establish God's kingdom on earth].

Some might think that the "man child" in verse 7, next, refers to Christ. Such is not the case. Mary brought forth Christ. The Church did not bring Christ forth. Rather, He brought forth the Church.

3 And she [*the Church, verse 7*] brought forth a man child [*verse 7, the kingdom of God*], who was to rule all nations with a rod of iron [*the word of God, 1 Nephi 11:25*]; and her child [*see verse 7, the kingdom of God and the righteous Saints who belong to it*] was caught up unto God and his throne [*the righteous are eventually taken up to live in celestial glory with God*].

4 And there appeared another sign [*John is seeing actual events in premortality and on earth in vision*] in heaven; and behold, a great red dragon [*Satan*], having seven heads [*symbolic of counterfeiting God's work*] and ten [*a number often associated with being well-organized*] horns [*horns are symbolic of power*], and seven crowns [*Satan has authority in his own realm*] upon his heads. And his tail drew the third part of the stars of heaven [*a third part of the premortal spirits in our group;*], and did cast them to the earth. And the dragon stood before the woman which was delivered [*gave birth to the Kingdom of God, verse 7*], ready to devour her child [*the Kingdom of God, verse 7*] after it was born. [*Satan has tried to destroy God's work from the beginning.*]

Apostle James E. Talmage indicates that there was a certain number of spirits assigned to our group to come to this earth. (See *Articles of Faith*, James E. Talmage, printed in 1977, p. 194.) Thus, we understand the "third part" in verse 4, above, to be a third part of our group of spirits.

5 And the woman fled into the wilderness [*symbolic of the Great Apostasy; the Church is gone for many centuries until the restoration by Joseph Smith*], where she had a place prepared of God, that they should feed [*nourish, take care of*] her there a thousand two hundred and threescore years.

6 And there was war in heaven [*a war of words, ideas, truth, error, loyalties, etc.*]; Michael [*Adam*] and his angels [*righteous spirits*] fought against the dragon [*Satan*]; and the dragon and his angels [*wicked spirits*] fought against Michael;

7 And the dragon [*Satan*] prevailed not [*did not win*] against Michael, neither the child [*the kingdom of our God*], nor the woman [*the Church*] which was the church of God, who had been delivered of her pains, and brought forth the kingdom of our God and his Christ. [*This is a great prophecy that Satan*

will not ultimately win against Christ and the forces of good.]

8 Neither was there place found in heaven for the great dragon [*Lucifer, Satan*], who was cast out; that old serpent called the devil, and also called Satan, which deceiveth the whole world; he was cast out into the earth; and his angels were cast out with him. [*They are here on earth and in the spirit world prison, tempting and fighting against that which is good. See* Teachings of Presidents of the Church, Brigham Young, *p. 282 (study course for priesthood and Relief Society).*]

9 And I heard a loud voice saying in heaven, Now is come salvation, and strength, and the kingdom of our God, and the power of his Christ; [*In other words, the earth is set up and "school is in session"; worthy spirits can go down to earth, have opportunities to choose between good and evil, join the kingdom of God via the gospel of Jesus Christ, and gain exaltation because of the Atonement of Christ–see verse 11.*]

10 For the accuser [*Satan*] of our brethren is cast down, which accused them before our God day and night [*continuously*].

11 For they [*the righteous*] have overcome him [*Satan*] by the blood of the Lamb [*using the Atonement of Christ*], and by the word of their testimony [*keeping their covenants*]; for they loved not their own lives, but kept the testimony even unto death [*endured faithful to the end*]. Therefore, rejoice O heavens, and ye that dwell in them [*righteous people bring joy to the inhabitants of heaven*].

12 And after these things I heard another voice saying, Woe to [*a warning, caution to*] the inhabiters of the earth, yea, and they who dwell upon the islands of the sea [*all continents; everybody on earth*]! for the devil is come down unto you, having great wrath, because he knoweth that he hath but a short time [*beware of Satan; he is really "turning up the heat"*].

13 For when the dragon [*Satan*] saw that he was cast unto the earth, he persecuted the woman [*the Church*] which brought forth the man child [*the kingdom of God—see verse 7*].

The "great eagle" in verse 14, next, could possibly symbolize the role that the United States of America would play in providing a safe place for the

Church to start and then grow when the time was right.

14 Therefore, to the woman were given two wings of a great eagle, that she might flee into the wilderness, into her place, where she is nourished for a time, and times, and half a time, from the face of the serpent [*Satan, who wants to destroy the Church in its infancy. See verse 4*].

15 And the serpent [*Satan*] casteth out of his mouth water as a flood [*a wicked flood of filthiness designed to get into every aspect of life. This may tie in with the "filthy water" in 1 Nephi 12:16*], after the woman [*the Church, verse 7*], that he might cause her to be carried away of the flood [*destroyed by a flood of wickedness*].

16 And the earth helpeth the woman [*example: Moses 6:63, "all things bear witness"*], and the earth openeth her mouth, and swalloweth up the flood which the dragon [*Satan*] casteth out of his mouth [*the earth is set up to help us overcome Satan and gain exaltation*].

17 Therefore, the dragon was wroth [*angry*] with the woman [*the Church*], and went to make war with the remnant of her seed [*the Saints in the last days*], which keep the commandments of God, and have the testimony of Jesus Christ [*who make and keep covenants with God*].

REVELATION 13

This chapter contains one of the most notable and often talked about topics in the Bible. It is usually referred to as "the mark of the beast" and is mentioned in verses 16 and 17.

We don't have exact interpretations of many of the things John saw in this chapter. It is easy to be caught up in trying to figure out details and thus miss the rather obvious and simple messages. For instance, we may not know who or what the beast is or what his seven heads and ten horns are. However, it is obvious that evil is being represented in the vision as vicious and destructive, something for us to avoid. The beast's seven heads might represent Satan's attempted counterfeits of God's perfect work since the number seven represents perfection in Bible symbolism. On the other hand, the seven heads could represent attempts by Lucifer to confuse us. (For example, which one is really Satan, or one of his front organizations?) Or perhaps the seven heads symbolize Satan's ability to come at us from several different directions, using many different types of temptations tailored specifically for us.

The head wounded, which was then healed in verse 3, could remind us that just when we think we have overcome one of Satan's temptations, he bounces back and tries for us again. The important thing is for us to be reminded that Satan is a very capable enemy and we must do all we can to avoid getting the mark of the beast in our foreheads (verse 16); in other words, to avoid becoming followers of Satan.

The heading to this chapter in the LDS English-speaking version of the Bible is very helpful. It says *"John sees fierce-looking beasts which represent degenerate earthly kingdoms controlled by Satan—The devil works miracles and deceives men."*

We will now proceed with our study of this chapter of John's Revelation. The JST makes significant changes to verse 1, next.

1 And I stood upon the sand of the sea, and saw a beast rise up

out of the sea, having seven heads and ten horns [*perhaps symbolizing that Satan is well-organized but not as powerful as Christ's 12 horns, 12 eyes, and 12 servants or Apostles in JST, 5:6*], and upon his horns ten crowns [*symbolizing power over kingdoms*], and upon his heads the name of blasphemy [*symbolic of total disrespect for God*].

JST Revelation 13:1

1 And I saw another sign, in the likeness of the kingdoms of the earth; a beast rise up out of the sea, and he stood upon the sand of the sea, having seven heads and ten horns; and upon his horns ten crowns; and upon his heads the name of blasphemy.

The phrase "sand of the sea" in the JST, above, reminds us that Satan's kingdom is built upon "sand." As depicted by the Savior in Matthew 7:24–27, sand is not a good foundation upon which to build. It will eventually crumble out from under the "kingdom" and the kingdom will be destroyed.

Next, in verse 2, fierce and powerful beasts known among biblical cultures to be destroyers among flocks depict Satan's degenerate earthly kingdoms.

2 And the beast which I saw was like unto a leopard, and his feet were as the feet of a bear, and his mouth as the mouth of a lion [*he has great ability to destroy*]: and the dragon [*the devil*] gave him [*Satan's degenerate earthly kingdoms*] his power, and his seat, and great authority.

3 And I saw one of his heads as it were wounded to death; and his deadly wound was healed: and all the world wondered after the beast [*the majority of the world will admire and desire wickedness in the last days*].

4 And they worshipped the dragon [*Satan*] which gave power unto the beast [*representing degenerate earthly kingdoms controlled by Satan; again, see heading to Revelation 13 in our English version of the Bible*]: and they [*the wicked*] worshipped the beast, saying, Who is like unto the beast? who is able to make war with him [*isn't he wonderful!*]?

The admiration and worshipping of wickedness, shown to John in verse 4, above, can apply to many aspects of our world today, including the admiration and near worship of crudeness, filth, cruelty, violence, sexual immorality, disloyalty to commitments, unfaithfulness to

spouse and family, political corruption, and so forth, as seen in media and lifestyles throughout our last-days' world.

Next, we see that Satan and his degenerate earthly kingdoms have great power.

5 And there was given unto him a mouth speaking great things and blasphemies [*God allows Satan to wield power that we might be properly tested*]; and power was given unto him to continue forty and two months. [*Forty-two months; a thousand two hundred and threescore days, similar to the time allocated to the two prophets in Revelation 11:3 to do God's work. Perhaps the use of 42 months again here simply implies that whenever God is doing His work, Satan is allowed to provide opposition at the same time. Such will be the case until the Millennium, during which he will be bound and "shall not have power to tempt any man" (D&C 101:28).*]

6 And he opened his mouth in blasphemy [*mocking God and all that is sacred and good*] against God, to blaspheme his name, and his tabernacle, and them that dwell in heaven. [*Satan and his followers will mock all that is sacred on earth and in heaven.*]

Some read verse 7, next, and think that Satan will eventually overcome all the righteous in the last days. Such is obviously not the case. They need to read verse 8 also, where we see that Satan overcomes only those who worship or follow him. In other words, he overcomes those who do not overcome him by following Christ and accessing His Atonement in their lives.

7 And it was given unto him [*allowed him*] to make war with the saints, and to overcome them [*remember, as mentioned above, only the unfaithful Saints whose names are not written in the book of life will be overcome; see verse 8*]: and power was given him over all kindreds, and tongues, and nations [*he is allowed to tempt people everywhere*].

At the risk of being redundant, we will again emphasize that Satan will not overcome all of the righteous. Note that "all," in verse 8, next, refers to those "whose names are not written in the book of the . . . Lamb," as defined in the note following verse 8.

8 And all [*the wicked*] that dwell upon the earth shall worship him, whose names are not written in the book of life of the Lamb slain from the foundation of the world [*those who do not follow the Savior are worshiping Satan; compare with Matthew 12:30*].

"The book of life of the Lamb" in verse 8, above, is symbolic of the record kept in heaven that contains the names of those who will be exalted. See D&C 132:19.

9 If any man have an ear, let him hear [*you would be very wise to heed these warnings about Satan*].

10 He [*the powerful wicked*] that leadeth into captivity shall go into captivity [*the wicked will be destroyed by the wicked; Mormon 4:5; also could mean that the wicked who lead others to the captivity of hell will go into the captivity of hell themselves*]: he [*the wicked*] that killeth with the sword must be [*will be*] killed with the sword. Here is the patience and the faith of the saints [*perhaps meaning that through being surrounded by opposition in the mortal world, the patience and faith of the Saints are developed*].

Among the messages we might glean from the next verses, we see that Satan and his followers do all in their power to replace Christ in the lives of people with counterfeits of their making. Some of these counterfeits will have tremendous power and influence among mankind.

11 And I beheld another beast coming up out of the earth; and he had two horns like a lamb [*"like a lamb," not "the Lamb," perhaps meaning a powerful false Christ, a counterfeit by Satan*], and he spake as a dragon [*like Satan; see Revelation 12:9*].

12 And he exerciseth all the power of the first beast before him [*Just when you think you've seen Satan or one of his representatives at his worst, worse will come!*], and causeth the earth and them [*the wicked*] which dwell therein to worship the first beast [*in verse 3, above*], whose deadly wound was healed.

13 And he doeth great wonders [*Satan and his angels can do miracles—see Revelation 16:14*], so that he maketh fire come down from heaven on the earth in the sight of men [*a counterfeit of Elijah's miracle, 1 Kings 18:38*],

14 And deceiveth them [*the wicked and foolish*] that dwell on the earth by the means of those miracles which he had power to do in the sight of the beast; saying to them that dwell on the earth,

that they should make an image to [*in other words, worship*] the beast, which had the wound by a sword, and did live. [*Satan will do all he can to get all people to follow him, to "worship" him by living wickedly in the last days.*]

15 And he had power to give life [*make wickedness attractive*] unto the image of the beast [*which the wicked made in verse 14 by following Satan's instructions*], that the image of the beast should both speak, and cause that as many as would not worship the image of the beast [*see explanation for verses 16–17, next*] should be killed [*people's "idols" can take over their lives and cause them to die spiritually, as well as physically in wars, plagues, etc. Also, the wicked can cause great trouble, temporarily, for the righteous*].

Verses 16 and 17, next, are an example of the importance of carefully considering context when interpreting verses of scripture. If one were to read only these two verses, the conclusion would be that, in the last days, "all" (verse 16) people will eventually come under the power of Satan and wicked people under his control. This would be very depressing and could cause people to give up hope. However, if we examine other verses in Revelation, we see the truth. For example, read Revelation 14:1, where we see 144,000 with the Father's name in their foreheads (symbolic of being righteous), rather than the mark of the beast in their foreheads. Furthermore, in Revelation 20:4, we see righteous people "which had not worshipped the beast, neither his image, neither had received his mark upon their foreheads, or in their hands." Thus, we see that all (Revelation 13:16) do not come under Satan's control, rather all the foolish or wicked do who "wondered after the beast" (verse 3).

In the culture of the Bible, "forehead" was symbolic of "loyalty." (See symbolism notes at the beginning of this study guide.) Thus, we see faithful Jews wearing phylacteries even today (see Bible Dictionary under "Phylacteries") tied to their foreheads, symbolizing loyalty and obedience to their God. Notice also in Revelation 14:1 that there are 144,000 righteous who have the "Father's name written in their foreheads," which symbolizes loyalty and obedience to the Father.

16 And he causeth all [*who follow Satan; the righteous are not part*

of this group because they have the seal of God in their foreheads as seen in Revelation 7:3], both small and great, rich and poor, free and bond, to receive a mark in their right hand, or in their foreheads [*symbolically indicating that they are loyal to Satan and the wickedness he sponsors*]:

17 And that no man might buy or sell, save he that had the mark, or the name of the beast, or the number of his name [*Satan exercises great control over economies where the majority are wicked or allow wickedness; the righteous today would do well to follow the counsel of the prophets regarding self-sufficiency and staying out of unnecessary debt, etc.*].

Verse 17, above, implies much of financial bondage in the last days. If we follow the council of the Brethren, we will not come under this bondage. For example, Elder L. Tom Perry counseled: "Live strictly within your income and save something for a rainy day. Incorporate in your lives the discipline of budgeting that which the Lord has blessed you with . . . avoid excessive debt. Necessary debt should be incurred only after careful, thoughtful prayer and after obtaining the best possible advice. We need the discipline to stay well within our ability to pay. Wisely, we have been counseled to avoid debt as we would avoid the plague. . . . It is so easy to allow consumer debt to get out of hand. If you do not have the discipline to control the use of credit cards, it is better not to have them. A well-managed family does not pay interest—it earns it. The definition I received from a wise boss at one time in my early business career was 'Thems that understands interest receives it, thems that don't pays it.' . . . Acquire and store a reserve of food and supplies that will sustain life. Obtain clothing and build a savings account on a sensible, well-planned basis that can serve well in times of emergency. As long as I can remember, we have been taught to prepare for the future and to obtain a year's supply of necessities. I would guess that the years of plenty have almost universally caused us to set aside this counsel. I believe the time to disregard this counsel is over. With events in the world today, it must be considered with all seriousness" (Perry, "If Ye Are Prepared Ye Shall Not Fear," *Ensign*, Nov. 1995, p. 36).

In verse 18, next, we encounter the rather elusive and famous "666." While there have been many attempts to explain what it might mean, and many attempts to apply it to particular individuals, the simple fact remains that we do not know what it means. In order to have this verse explained, we will have to wait for additional revelation from God through His authorized prophets, or a revelation from the Savior Himself during the Millennium when He will "reveal all things" (D&C 101:32).

18 Here is wisdom. Let him that hath understanding count the number of the beast: for it is the number of a man; and his number is Six hundred threescore and six [*in other words, 666*].

REVELATION 14

This chapter is in rather stark contrast to chapter 13, above. Whereas Satan and his degenerate front organizations, with powerful and influential wicked leaders, exert horribly effective influence among the inhabitants of the earth in the portion of the vision John saw, recorded in chapter 13, chapter 14 shows that large numbers of the righteous can and will triumph over Satan's gross wickedness.

In this chapter, verse 1, the Apostle John sees the Savior in glorious triumph standing with 144,000 righteous and pure high priests (D&C 77:11; Revelation 7:4; 14:1) who have the name of the Father written in their foreheads. This is in contrast to the wicked in chapter 13 who have the mark of the beast in their foreheads. In verses 2–5, he sees additional righteous followers of Christ who have prevailed over the devil and his wicked followers. He sees the restoration of the gospel in the last days (verses 6–7), and then sees the fall of Satan's kingdom (verses 8–11), including the final gathering of the righteous and the destruction of the wicked (verses 14–20).

1 And I [*John*] looked, and, lo, a Lamb [*Christ*] stood on the mount Sion [*this is representative of many appearances of the Savior before the actual Second Coming; D&C 133:18–20*], and with him an hundred forty and four thousand [*Revelation 7:4; 14:1; D&C 133:17–18*], having his Father's name written in their foreheads [*symbolizing that they were loyal to the Father*].

JST Revelation 14:1

1 And I looked, and, lo, a Lamb stood on the mount Sion, and with him a hundred forty and four thousand, having his Father's name written in their foreheads.

Did you have a difficult time finding the JST change in verse 1, above? This is one of those cases where the Prophet simply changed one word, "an" to "a," so that it now reads "a hundred forty and four thousand."

2 And I heard a voice from heaven, as the voice of many waters [*D&C 110:3*], and as the voice of a great thunder [*symbolic of a voice from heaven as on Sinai; Exodus 19:16–19*]: and I heard the voice of harpers harping with their harps [*in Bible symbolism, harps are symbolic of heaven*]:

3 And they sung as it were a new song [*one that couldn't be sung before the Millennium and the destruction of the wicked came; see note preceding Revelation 5:9 in this study guide*] before the throne [*in front of the throne of God*], and before the four beasts, and the elders: and no man could learn that song but the hundred and forty and four thousand [*plus many others as mentioned in Revelation 7:9*], which were redeemed from the earth. [*In other words,*

only the righteous, those who were saved by the Atonement, could sing the words of the new song, whose words applied to them, in the presence of God in celestial splendor. The words of the new song are, in effect, given in D&C 84:99–102.]

4 These are they which were not defiled with women [*they are morally clean*]; for they are virgins [*pure and clean, keeping the law of chastity; does not mean unmarried*]. These are they which follow the Lamb whithersoever he goeth [*who follow Christ at all costs*]. These were redeemed from among men, being the first-fruits [*the highest quality fruit; those who will attain exaltation*] unto God and to the Lamb.

5 And in their mouth was found no guile [*deceit; Strong's, #1388*]: for they are without fault [*blameless; without sin, pure and clean because of the Atonement*] before the throne of God.

6 And I saw another angel [*Angel Moroni plus many other angels who helped with the restoration; D&C 128:20–21; 133:36*] fly in the midst of heaven, having the everlasting gospel to preach unto them that dwell on the earth, and to every nation, and kindred, and

tongue, and people [*the restoration of the Church*],

7 Saying with a loud voice, Fear [*respect, reverence; Strong's, #5399*] God, and give glory to him; for the hour of his judgment is come: and worship him that made heaven, and earth, and the sea, and the fountains of waters.

Throughout the ages, sincere and righteous followers of the Savior have hoped for and looked forward to the day when Satan's kingdom will fall and wickedness will cease. Next, in verses 8–11, John is shown in vision that this will finally take place, in conjunction with the Second Coming of Christ, when the righteous can finally sing the new song referred to in verse 3, above.

8 And there followed another angel, saying, Babylon [*symbolic of Satan and his earthly kingdom*] is fallen, is fallen, that great city [*Satan's kingdom*], because she made all nations drink of the wine of [*the results of*] the wrath of her fornication.

"Wine," as used in verse 8, above, can have many symbolic meanings. For example, it can mean that Satan "intoxicates" people with wickedness. It can also mean that, just as wine is an intentional product, planned and produced, so also is wickedness an intentional product of the devil, planned, produced, and offered to all nations to lure them away from God.

"Fornication," as used at the end of verse 8, above, is often used in scripture in its wider sense to mean apostasy (see Bible Dictionary under "Adultery"), disloyalty, all manner of wickedness, breaking of covenants and commitments, and so forth.

The law of justice is explained in verses 9 and 10, next.

9 And the third angel followed them, saying with a loud voice, If any man worship the beast and his image [*Revelation 13:14*], and receive his mark in his forehead, or in his hand [*in other words, uses his agency to chose to be a loyal follower of Satan and the wickedness he sponsors*],

10 The same shall drink of the wine [*results of, punishments*] of the wrath of God, which is poured out without mixture [*undiluted*] into the cup of his indignation; and he [*the wicked*] shall be tormented with fire and brimstone in the presence of the holy angels, and in the presence of the Lamb [*will not be able to stand the presence of God; D&C 88:22*]:

11 And the smoke of their torment ascendeth up for ever and ever: and they have no rest day nor night, who worship the beast and his image, and whosoever receiveth the mark of his name [*applies eternally only to the sons of perdition, D&C 76:33; all other unrepentant wicked will eventually suffer for their own sins, D&C 19:17, and then be redeemed into the telestial kingdom—see D&C 76:103; Revelation 22:15*].

Next, in verses 12–13, we are taught the eternal truth that righteousness ultimately pays off wonderfully!

12 Here is the patience of the saints [*when the righteous see the fall of Satan's kingdom as mentioned in the above verses, they will see that their patience, in living the gospel and waiting for God to destroy Lucifer's kingdom, has paid off*]: here are they that keep the commandments of God, and the faith of Jesus.

13 And I heard a voice from heaven saying unto me, Write, Blessed are the dead which die in the Lord [*who have lived righteously*] from henceforth: Yea, saith the Spirit, that they may rest from their labours; and their works do follow them [*they will be rewarded for their righteousness*].

14 And I looked, and behold a white cloud [*symbolic of heaven*], and upon the cloud one [*Christ*] sat like unto the Son of man [*Christ*], having on his head a golden crown [*celestial*], and in his hand a sharp sickle [*it is "harvest" time*].

The phrase "like unto the Son of man," in verse 14, above, is explained in two notes following Revelation 1:13 in this study guide.

15 And another angel came out of the temple [*where Heavenly Father is; Revelation 3:12; 7:15*], crying with a loud voice to him [*Christ*] that sat on the cloud [*giving instructions to the Savior from the Father*], Thrust in thy sickle, and reap: for the time is come for thee to reap; for the harvest of the earth is ripe ["*the field is white already to harvest," D&C 6:3; in other words, the Father is telling Christ that it is time for the final gathering, prior to the Second Coming*].

First, the righteous are gathered out of all the earth.

16 And he [*Christ*] that sat on the cloud thrust in his sickle on the earth; and the earth was reaped [*Christ supervised the final gathering of the righteous; compare*

with D&C 86:7, in which the "wheat" is gathered first, and then the "tares" are burned. (This is a correction to the Bible, Matthew 13:30, which has the tares being gathered first.)].

Now the wicked will be "harvested" and cast into the fire. See verses 18 and 19.

17 And another angel [*the destroying angel; see verses 18–20*] came out of the temple [*from the presence of the Father*] which is in heaven, he also having a sharp sickle.

18 And another angel came out from the altar [*from the presence of the Father*], which had power over fire; and cried with a loud cry to him [*the destroying angel in verse 17*] that had the sharp sickle, saying, Thrust in thy sharp sickle, and gather the clusters of the vine of the earth; for her grapes [*wicked people*] are fully ripe [*ripe in iniquity, thoroughly wicked*].

19 And the angel thrust in his sickle into the earth, and gathered the vine of the earth [*the wicked*], and cast it into the great winepress of the wrath of God [*the destruction of the wicked—see D&C 133:50–51*].

It was just outside the city walls of Jerusalem, in Gethsemane and on Calvary, that the Savior's atoning blood was shed to redeem all who will repent from their sins. So also, in the vision, John saw the final battles in the last days where "all nations shall be engaged at Jerusalem" (heading to Zechariah 12 in the LDS English version of the Bible), resulting in an unimaginable river of blood of the wicked who now face the wrath and judgments of God. It would seem that "without the city" (verse 20) can symbolically represent the rest of the world of the wicked, who now face the realities of the law of justice, having rejected the law of mercy by their choice of intentional wickedness.

20 And the winepress was trodden without the city [*outside the city of Jerusalem*], and blood came out of the winepress [*D&C 133:50*], even unto the horse bridles [*in the vision, the river of blood of the wicked was deep enough to come up to the bridles on horses; in other words, many wicked are destroyed in the final terrible battles preceding the Second Coming, culminating with the destruction of the rest of the wicked when the Savior actually comes*], by the space of a thousand and six hundred furlongs [*the river of blood ran for about 200 miles in the vision seen by John; symbolic of terrible destruction accompanying the Battle of Armageddon and the Second Coming*].

JST Revelation 14:20

20 And the winepress was trodden without the city, and blood came out of the winepress, even unto the horses' bridles, by the space of a thousand and six hundred furlongs.

REVELATION 15

Have you noticed the "comparison and contrast" teaching method employed in this vision? Through John's inspired recording of his vision, we are shown a number of times the terrible fate of the wicked and then the joyous final state of the righteous. This chapter employs this approach again.

After a quick segment of the vision, recorded in verse 1, where John is shown that there are seven final plagues before the Second Coming, we see a beautiful part of the vision (verses 2–4) in which he was shown the reward of the righteous who overcame evil through the Atonement of Jesus Christ. He sees them on "a sea of glass," representing a celestial world (D&C 77:1 and 130:7), with "harps," symbolizing that they spend the rest of eternity in the presence of God. They are singing "the song of Moses . . . and the song of the Lamb" (verse 3), meaning that they have received the same reward that Moses receives from Christ and His Father (in other words, exaltation). Some of the words they "sing" in verses three and four are contained in our hymn "How Wondrous and Great."

After the beauties of eternal life for the righteous (verses 2–4), the vision proceeds and introduces the final seven plagues before the Millennium (verses 5–8).

There are no JST changes for this chapter.

1 And I saw another sign in heaven, great and marvellous, seven angels having the seven last plagues [*as described in chapters 16, 17, and 18, and which will take place prior to the Millennium*]; for in them is filled up [*concluded; completed*] the wrath of God.

Remember that the number seven represents completeness or perfection in biblical symbolism. With this in mind, we can see that the seven angels who have the seven

remaining plagues symbolize the perfection and completeness of God's perfect judgments against the wicked in the final windup scenes before the Savior's Second Coming. As stated at the end of verse 1, above, the wrath of God against the wicked is "filled up" or perfectly finished in preparation for the Millennium to begin.

2 And I saw as it were a sea of glass mingled with fire [*celestial glory; D&C 130:7*]: and them [*the righteous*] that had gotten the victory over the beast [*in chapter 13*], *and over his image [13:14*], and over his mark [*13:16–17*], and over the number of his name [*13:17–18; in other words, the righteous who had overcome all attempts of Satan to trap them*], stand on the sea of glass, having the harps of God [*symbolizing that they were standing in the presence of God; among other things, the harps could symbolize that they were found in "harmony" with God*].

Next in the vision, as mentioned in the introduction to this chapter, above, John is shown the righteous (verse 2) being able to rejoice because they have received the same righteous rewards of celestial glory and exaltation over which Moses rejoiced.

3 And they sing the song of Moses the servant of God [*they sing God's praises like Moses did*], and the song of the Lamb [*Christ*], saying, Great and marvellous are thy works, Lord God Almighty; just and true are thy ways, thou King of saints [*praising God*].

4 Who shall not fear thee, O Lord, and glorify thy name? for thou only art holy: for all nations shall come and worship before thee; for thy judgments are made manifest.

5 And after that I looked, and, behold, the temple of the tabernacle of the testimony in heaven was opened [*see note for Revelation 11:19 in this study guide*]:

6 And the seven angels came out of the temple, having the seven plagues [*spoken of in verse 1*], clothed in pure and white linen [*celestial beings—fine linen represents personal righteousness in Revelation 19:8*], and having their breasts girded with golden girdles [*symbolic of the best, celestial*].

7 And one of the four beasts [*Revelation 4:6*] gave unto the seven angels seven golden vials [*representing the final seven*

plagues] full of the wrath of God, who liveth for ever and ever.

8 And the temple was filled with smoke [*symbolic of God's glory as on Sinai; Exodus 19:18*] from the glory of God, and from his power; and no man was able to enter into the temple, till the seven plagues of the seven angels were fulfilled [*in other words, millennial conditions won't start until the final seven plagues are finished*].

REVELATION 16

This chapter (along with chapters 17 and 18) will review the devastating "seven last plagues" (Revelation 15:1), which will sweep the earth leading up to the Battle of Armageddon and the Second Coming of Christ. A major message here is that there will be widespread destruction before the Millennium.

You will see that this part of John's vision indicates that there will be terrible damage to the ecology of the earth in the last days prior to the Second Coming. These plagues will include great damage to the land (the earth, verse 2), the sea (verse 3), the rivers (verse 4), the sun (verse 8), Satan's kingdom (the wicked, verse 10), and the air (verse 17).

1 And I [*John*] heard a great voice [*possibly the voice of Heavenly Father*] out of the temple [*from heaven*] saying to the seven angels [*mentioned in Revelation 15:6–8*], Go your ways, and pour out the vials [*small bowls; containers for liquids*] of the wrath of God upon the earth [*start the final plagues*].

2 And the first [*angel*] went, and poured out his vial [*the first plague during the final scenes*] upon the earth; and there fell a noisome [*destructive: Strong's, #2556*] and grievous [*evil, devastating; Strong's, #4190*] sore upon the men which [*who*] had the mark of the beast [*who were loyal to Satan, evil, wickedness*], and upon them which worshipped his image.

Did you notice that the plague in verse 2, above, is directed at the wicked, those who have the mark of the beast upon them (discussed more in Revelation 13:16–17) and who worship his image? This can be a source of encouragement for those who are striving to be righteous, who, in considerable measure, will be protected during the tumultuous times spoken of in this chapter. The Lord explains:

D&C 97:22–26

22 For behold, and lo, vengeance cometh speedily upon the ungodly as the whirlwind; and who shall escape it?

23 The Lord's scourge shall pass over by night and by day, and the report thereof shall vex all people; yea, it shall not be stayed until the Lord come;

24 For the indignation of the Lord is kindled against their abominations and all their wicked works.

25 Nevertheless, Zion shall escape if she observe to do all things whatsoever I have commanded her.

26 But if she observe not to do whatsoever I have commanded her, I will visit her according to all her works, with sore affliction, with pestilence, with plague, with sword, with vengeance, with devouring fire.

Just one example of the protection provided to the righteous by the Lord during these final scenes of the earth's history might be the relative security for members of the Church who follow the counsel of our prophets, seers, and revelators regarding provident living.

3 And the second angel poured

out his vial [*the second plague*] upon the sea; and it became as the blood [*similar to the plague of blood in Egypt; Exodus 7:20*] of a dead man [*in other words, the waters were polluted, like a corpse*]: and every living soul died in the sea.

In addition to literal destructive pollution of the seas in the last days and other sources of destruction upon the seas (compare D&C 61:4–5), verse 3, above, may refer to the floods of wickedness sponsored by the devil in the last days, as mentioned in Revelation 17:15.

4 And the third angel poured out his vial [*the third plague*] upon the rivers and fountains of waters [*springs*]; and they became blood [*similar to the plague in Exodus 7:19–21*].

5 And I heard the angel of the waters [*the angel who poured the plague upon the waters in verse 4, above*] say, Thou art righteous, O Lord, which art, and wast, and shalt be, because thou hast judged thus. [*This punishment is fair and just because of the wickedness of men.*]

6 For they have shed the blood of saints and prophets, and thou hast given them blood to drink [*symbolic of forbidden evils, pollution; in other words, this is the law of the harvest; what you have planted comes back to you at harvest time or Judgment Day*]; for they are worthy [*they deserve such punishment*].

7 And I heard another out of the altar [*from heaven; Revelation 8:3*] say, Even so, Lord God Almighty, true and righteous are thy judgments. [*In other words, a second witness, according to the law of witnesses, that God is completely fair and just in punishing the wicked.*]

JST Revelation 16:7

7 And I heard another angel who came out from the altar saying, Even so, Lord God Almighty, true and righteous are thy judgments.

8 And the fourth angel poured out his vial [*plague*] upon the sun; and power was given unto him to scorch men with fire [*perhaps similar to our modern saying, "turn up the heat," to see if we can get some of them to repent*].

Sadly, according to John's vision, most of the wicked in the last days will not repent despite the terrible calamities and punishments of God that come upon them.

9 And men were scorched with great heat [*terrible calamities*], and blasphemed [*mocked*] the name of God, which hath power over these plagues [*God could stop these plagues if men would repent*]: and they repented not to give him glory.

10 And the fifth angel poured out his vial [*the fifth plague*] upon the seat [*headquarters*] of the beast [*Satan*]; and his kingdom was full of [*spiritual*] darkness; and they [*the wicked*] gnawed their tongues for [*because of*] pain [*the wicked will suffer greatly, both physically and spiritually, because they refuse to repent and let Christ's Atonement pay for their sins; D&C 19:15–18*],

11 And blasphemed [*mocked*] the God of heaven because of their pains and their sores, and repented not of their deeds [*their wickedness*].

12 And the sixth angel poured out his vial [*the sixth plague*] upon the great river Euphrates [*runs through modern-day Iraq and into the Persian Gulf*]; and the water thereof was dried up, that the way of the kings of the east might be prepared [*perhaps*

symbolic of world leaders gathering for the Battle of Armageddon; see verse 16, below].

You may wish to glance back in this study guide to the JST of Revelation 9:14 where you will see that Joseph Smith replaced "great river Euphrates" with "the bottomless pit." With that in mind, "the great river Euphrates," in verse 12, above, could symbolize that that geographic area of the world will be a major influential component of Satan's kingdom in the last days before the Second Coming.

13 And I saw three unclean [*evil*] spirits like frogs [*frogs represent unclean spirits in some cultures; perhaps this goes back to the plague of frogs in Egypt, Exodus 8:6, with the same purpose, i.e., to encourage people to repent and obey God*] come out of the mouth of the dragon [*Satan; Revelation 12:9*], and out of the mouth of the beast, and out of the mouth of the false prophet [*evil spirits are much involved in all Satan-sponsored evil and wickedness*].

14 For they are the spirits of devils, working miracles [*Satan and his evil spirits have much power, although limited by God*], which go forth unto the kings

[*wicked political leaders*] of the earth and of the whole world, to gather them to the battle of that great day of God Almighty [*the battle of Armageddon; see verse 16*].

15 Behold, I [*Christ*] come as a thief [*unexpectedly; will catch the wicked off guard, but not the righteous, D&C 106:4–5*]. Blessed is he that watcheth, and keepeth his garments [*who keeps himself unspotted from the sins of the world (D&C 59:9); who keeps clean via the Atonement*], lest he walk naked [*his wickedness is no longer "covered" by excuses on Judgment Day; compare with 2 Nephi 9:14*], and they see his shame [*embarrassment for his wicked deeds*].

16 And he [*perhaps referring back to the "dragon" (Satan) in verse 13*] gathered them together into a place called in the Hebrew tongue Armageddon [*also called "Megiddo," geographically located today in a valley about 60 miles north of Jerusalem in northern Israel*].

17 And the seventh angel [*probably Adam; see D&C 88:110 and 112*] poured out his vial [*plague*] into the air; and there came a great voice [*Heavenly Father's voice*]

out of the temple of heaven, from the throne, saying, It is done [*the end is here; Revelation 11:15*].

18 And there were voices, and thunders, and lightnings; and there was a great earthquake [*great destruction, perhaps including that which was caused by putting the land masses back together; D&C 133:23–24*], such as was not since men were upon the earth, so mighty an earthquake, and so great [*final destruction before the Millennium*].

19 And the great city [*Babylon, Satan's kingdom; see middle of this verse*] was divided into three parts [*perhaps meaning 1/3, 1/3, and 1/3, symbolic of Satan and his 1/3 completely dominating the wicked in the last days*], and the cities of the nations fell [*all worldly kingdoms have fallen; "a full end of all nations"(see D&C 87:6)*]: and great Babylon came in remembrance before God [*the time for God's full punishments upon Babylon arrived in the vision*], to give unto her the cup of the wine of the fierceness of his wrath [*gave the wicked the punishments they had earned*].

20 And every island fled away, and the mountains were not found

[geographical changes in conjunction with the Second Coming and the earth's paradisiacal glory at the beginning of the Millennium; D&C 133:22–24; tenth article of faith].

Verse 21, next, seems to be a review of one of the final destructions of the wicked before the beginning of the Millennium and would seem to fit before or in conjunction with verse 20, above.

21 And there fell upon men a great hail out of heaven, every stone about the weight of a talent *[in Old Testament weight, about 75 pounds (see Bible Dictionary, p. 789), but we don't know what a talent was in New Testament times]*: and men blasphemed *[mocked and criticized]* God *[they didn't repent]* because of the plague of the hail; for the plague thereof was exceeding great.

REVELATION 17

The description of the final seven plagues mentioned in Revelation 15:1 is continued here. This chapter of Revelation makes use of many symbols and images introduced previously in the vision. If you have become somewhat familiar with many of them,

studying this part of the vision will be a rather rewarding experience, as far as understanding biblical symbolism is concerned. In it, we see "the great whore" (Satan, in verse 1) sitting on the "many waters" (representing the wicked in all nations; verse 15). By this point in John's vision, the devil has been highly successful among the leaders and inhabitants of the earth, and they are "drunk" (out of control) with wickedness (verse 2). The woman in verse 3 is the complete opposite of the woman (the Church) in JST Revelation 12:7, symbolizing Satan's skill at being alluring, seductive, and at the same time attractive while blaspheming and prostituting all that is good, pure, and righteous. The beast ridden by the woman has "seven heads" and "ten horns" (Revelation 13:1), symbolizing, among other things, Satan's counterfeiting of God's work and his power to attack us from several different directions.

The woman in this chapter has "MYSTERY" (Secret combinations—see footnote 5a in your English version of the LDS Bible) written upon her forehead (forehead here symbolizes loyalty, dedication to Satan's goals) along with several other terms describing Satan's kingdom. In verse 8 we see the wicked, those "whose names were not written in the book of life," astonished that "the beast . . . was, and is not," perhaps meaning that Babylon was once powerful, but now is not; in other words, has fallen at the Second Coming. At the end of verse 8, these same wicked are astonished "when they behold the beast that was, and is not, and yet is," perhaps meaning Satan's kingdom was here, but is not here now, yet is still in existence in outer darkness (after the final battle at the end of the Millennium).

In verse 16, the ten horns take on additional symbolic identity as parts of Satan's kingdom which "hate the whore and . . . make her desolate and naked, and shall eat her flesh, and burn her with fire." In other words, "That great and abominable church, which is the whore of all the earth, shall turn upon their own heads; for they shall war among themselves" (1 Nephi 22:13).

A very comforting prophetic fact in verse 14 is that "the Lamb (Christ) shall overcome them (the wicked, including Satan and his evil spirits)." Thus, those who remain faithful to the Lord are assured that they will be on the winning side.

With the above background to this chapter in mind, let's go ahead and watch this part of the vision via John's inspired record.

1 And there came one of the seven angels [*Revelation 15:1*] which had the seven vials [*representing the final seven plagues before the Millennium*], and talked with me [*John*], saying unto me, Come hither; I will shew unto thee the judgment [*punishment*] of the great whore [*a word that brings to mind the word "prostitution," and means perversion, terrible abuse of that which is good, apostasy from the gospel of Jesus Christ, and all else that is good and honorable, and so forth; the great whore is the church or kingdom of the devil; 1 Nephi 14:10–11*], that sitteth upon many waters [*representing peoples and nations of the earth; Revelation 17:15*]:

2 With whom the [*wicked*] kings [*leaders*] of the earth have committed fornication [*they have "stepped out" on the true God, have been unfaithful to Him*], and the inhabitants of the earth have been made drunk [*gone out of control*] with the wine [*symbolizing the attractiveness of Satan's temptations*] of her fornication [*terrible wickedness of all kinds*].

Remember that the term "fornication," as used in verse 2, above, and elsewhere in this chapter, refers back to the "great whore" in verse 1, and is often used to mean wickedness of all types, as explained in the Bible Dictionary (at the back of your English version of the LDS Bible) under "Adultery." Two other examples of this usage of the term are found in Jeremiah 3:8 and Revelation 14:8.

3 So he [*one of the seven angels*] carried me away in the spirit into the wilderness [*the apostate world*]: and I saw a woman [*symbolizing Satan's counterfeits for the true Church, which was represented by a righteous woman in JST Revelation 12:1 and 7*] sit upon a scarlet [*symbolic of royalty, governing power*] coloured beast [*the beast is controlled by Satan; see Revelation 13 heading*], full of names of blasphemy [*full of mocking, disrespect for God, sacred things, truth, chastity, etc.*], having seven heads and ten horns [*the number ten, in biblical symbolism, represents ordinal perfection, i.e., well-ordered or well organized; in other words, Satan's kingdom is well organized; horns symbolize power*].

4 And the woman was arrayed [*dressed*] in purple and scarlet colour, and decked with gold and precious stones and pearls [*all symbolic of royalty, wealth, power, glory, materialism, etc., i.e., Satan's kingdom can be very attractive and has its "hour of glory" on the earth*], having a golden cup [*counterfeiting God's "best"*] in her hand full of abominations and filthiness [*the things Satan "pours" out upon the earth*] of her fornication:

5 And upon her forehead was a name written, MYSTERY [*secret combinations*], BABYLON THE GREAT [*Satan and his kingdom; Isaiah 14:4 and 12*], THE MOTHER OF HARLOTS [*the "producer of terrible wickedness"; just as a harlot, prostitute, appears desirable to wicked men, so also Satan's ways appear desirable to the wicked*] AND ABOMINATIONS OF THE EARTH.

6 And I saw the woman drunken with the blood of the saints [*Satan's forces have caused much suffering for the Saints, who strive to keep their lives in harmony with God's laws*], and with the blood of the martyrs of Jesus: and when I saw her, I wondered [*marveled; Strong's, #2296*] with great admiration [*surprise, astonishment; see Revelation 17:6, footnote c, in our English LDS Bible*].

7 And the angel said unto me, Wherefore didst thou marvel [*why were you so astonished*]? I will tell [*explain to*] thee the mystery of the woman, and of the beast [*also mentioned in Revelation 13*] that carrieth her, which hath the seven heads and ten horns.

8 The beast [*Satan and his forces; Revelation 9:1–2*] that thou sawest was, and is not [*see possible interpretation of this phrase in the introduction to this chapter, above*]; and shall ascend out of the bottomless pit, and go into perdition [*Revelation 20:1–3; D&C 76:26*]: and they that dwell on the earth shall wonder [*will be amazed when they see Satan and his forces trimmed down to size as told in Isaiah 14:12–16*], whose names were not written in the book of life [*in other words, the wicked*] from the foundation of the world [*because of disobedience to the gospel which was established before the foundation of the world*], when they behold the beast that was, and is not, and yet is [*perhaps meaning Satan was here on earth, is not here anymore, because he is in perdition at this point of the vision*].

9 And here is the mind which hath wisdom [*if you have wisdom, you will understand this*]. The

seven heads are seven mountains [*some Bible scholars believe that this could refer to Rome, which persecuted the Saints in John's day, but such an interpretation is likely far too limited; see also notes in verse 18*], on which the woman sitteth.

We don't know the interpretation of many of the following images and events in John's vision. Therefore, there is wisdom in following Alma's approach to such things.

Alma 37:11

11 Now these mysteries are not yet fully made known unto me; therefore I shall forbear.

10 And there are seven kings: five are fallen, and one is, and the other is not yet come; and when he cometh, he must continue a short space.

11 And the beast that was, and is not, even he is the eighth, and is of the seven, and goeth into perdition.

12 And the ten horns which thou sawest are ten kings, which have received no kingdom as yet; but receive power as kings one hour with the beast [*perhaps meaning that they will have temporary power and glory in Satan's organizations*].

13 These have one mind [*perhaps meaning they are united in evil*], and shall give their power and strength [*loyalty*] unto the beast.

14 These shall make war with the Lamb [*Christ*], and the Lamb shall overcome them [*a wonderfully comforting statement of eternal fact*]: for he is Lord of lords, and King of kings: and they that are with him are called, and chosen [*a word meaning "elected" by God for eternal happiness*], and faithful.

> As stated in verse 14, above, Christ is "Lord of lords, and King of kings." It is interesting to note that "Lord" with a capital "L" refers to Christ, as does "King" with a capital "K." The righteous, who will rule with Him during the Millennium, are the "lords" and "kings," spelled with small "l" and small "k."

15 And he saith unto me, The waters [*verse 1*] which thou sawest, where the whore sitteth, are peoples, and multitudes, and nations, and tongues.

> Just as water gets into everything—for instance, when a home's basement is flooded—so also the "waters," symbolizing a flood of wickedness in the last days, get into all aspects of society.

16 And the ten horns which thou sawest upon the beast, these shall hate the whore, and shall make her desolate and naked, and shall eat her flesh, and burn her with fire [*perhaps a reminder that Satan's followers often turn on each other; Isaiah 49:26; Mormon 4:5*].

17 For God hath put in their [*the wicked*] hearts to fulfil his [*Satan's?*] will, and to agree, and give their kingdom unto the beast, until the words of God shall be fulfilled [*until the Millennium comes and judgment catches up with the wicked*].

> The phrase "for God hath put in their hearts" in verse 17, above, is probably a mistranslation similar to Exodus 4:21 in which the Lord is reported to have said regarding Pharaoh, "I will harden his heart." It was corrected in the JST to read "but Pharaoh will harden his heart." God does not inspire people to do evil; rather, He allows them agency to choose between good and evil.

18 And the woman which thou sawest is that great city, which reigneth over the kings of the earth [*this city could be Rome in John's day, but in a general sense would seem more likely to symbolize "Babylon" or the*

"church of the devil" as stated in 1 Nephi 14:10–11].

REVELATION 18

This chapter continues the description (begun in chapter 16 and continued in chapter 17) of the final seven plagues leading up to the destruction of the wicked and the beginning of the Millennium.

Chapter 17 gave considerable detail about Babylon, which is Satan and his wicked earthly kingdom. Now, in chapter 18, John sees the fall of Babylon, described as "the woman . . . that great city" in Revelation 17:18. The actual ancient city of Babylon is used often in scripture to symbolize Satan's huge kingdom. Babylon was an enormous city, straddling the Euphrates River, and was said to have had walls 335 feet high, 85 feet wide, and 56 miles long surrounding the square city (see Bible Dictionary under "Babylon").

One of the sad things in this part of John's vision is that the wicked who "have committed fornication and lived deliciously (in lustful, riotous sin) with her (Babylon)" will mourn Babylon's downfall

instead of repenting and worrying about their status with God. See verses 10–19. They have no "godly sorrow" as described in 2 Corinthians 7:10.

There are no JST changes for this chapter.

1 And after these things I saw another angel come down from heaven, having great power; and the earth was lightened [*brightened, lit up*] with his glory.

Have you noticed the strong emphasis in this part of John's vision that wickedness does not pay? The unrepentant wicked will absolutely have to face the consequences of their wicked and selfish choices. In verse 2, next, we see this fact strongly emphasized once again.

2 And he cried mightily with a strong voice, saying, Babylon the great is fallen, is fallen [*Satan's kingdom on earth has come to an end via the Second Coming*], and is [*has*] become the habitation of [*dwelling place for*] devils, and the hold [*prison; Strong's, #5438*] of every foul [*wicked*] spirit, and a cage [*prison; the unrighteous have been "caged" by their wickedness and ultimately "trapped" by Satan*] of every unclean and hateful [*detestable; Strong's,*

#3404] bird [*the wicked are destroyed and are turned over to Satan to pay for their own sins; 2 Nephi 12:10, D&C 101:24, 19:17*].

3 For all nations have drunk of the wine [*intentionally and skillfully produced temptations of the devil*] of the wrath of her fornication [*people in all nations of the earth have joined Satan's kingdom, Babylon, in gross wickedness and disloyalty to God*], and the kings [*leaders, people of power and influence*] of the earth have committed fornication [*gross wickedness; symbolic of stepping out on God, breaking covenants and promises, going against conscience, extreme disloyalty to that which is good and right*] with her, and the merchants of the earth are waxed [*have grown*] rich through the abundance of her ["*Babylon's*"] delicacies [*in other words, much wealth has been acquired by exploiting people's wicked and lustful desires*].

Next, in verses 4–5, we see a tender, passionate invitation and warning directed to the people of the Lord to avoid the widespread sin and pitfalls of wickedness prevalent during the final plagues of the last days. We feel the love of God and hear much of this type of message from our church leaders, especially during general conferences.

4 And I heard another voice from heaven, saying, Come out of her, my people, that ye be not partakers of her sins, and that ye receive not of her plagues [*the righteous are warned not to participate in the gross evils of the last days*].

5 For her sins have reached unto heaven, and God hath remembered her iniquities. [*God is fully aware of what is going on and Babylon will fall and the wicked will be punished.*]

6 Reward her even as she rewarded you [*this is the law of the harvest; in other words, "whatsoever ye sow, that shall ye also reap" (D&C 6:33)*], and double unto her double according to her works: in the cup which she hath filled fill to her double [*Babylon's cup of wickedness is completely full, therefore, punish her and her followers accordingly*].

7 How much [*to the degree that*] she hath glorified herself, and lived deliciously [*wickedly, riotously*], so much [*to the same degree*] torment and sorrow give her [*an equation of justice; D&C 1:10*]: for she [*Babylon; the wicked*] saith in her heart [*the wicked fool themselves by thinking . . .*], I sit a

queen [*I am untouchable, I have great power*], and am no widow [*I won't be cut off from support and admiration*], and shall see no sorrow [*I won't get caught up with or be punished*].

8 Therefore shall [*this is why*] her plagues come in one day [*in other words, suddenly*], death, and mourning, and famine; and she shall be utterly burned with fire [*the wicked will be burned at the Second Coming, utterly destroyed by the Savior's glory; D&C 5:19; 2 Nephi 12:10, 19, 21*]: for strong [*powerful*] is the Lord God who judgeth her [*God has power over Satan*].

9 And the kings [*powerful, wicked leaders*] of the earth, who have committed fornication [*who have been extremely wicked*] and lived deliciously [*riotously*] with her [*the whore, Satan's kingdom, Babylon*], shall bewail her [*mourn losing her; Strong's, #2799*], and lament for her [*instead of repenting*], when they shall see the smoke of her burning [*the wicked will be devastated by the destruction of their lifestyle*],

As mentioned previously, it is tragic that the wicked spoken of in this part of the vision do not repent when they see the collapse of their lifestyles and associations with Babylon.

Instead, they are aghast at the downfall of the devil's kingdom and their pleasures associated with it.

10 Standing afar off for the fear of her torment, saying, Alas, alas, that great city Babylon, that mighty city! for in one hour is thy judgment come. [*The Second Coming will change things quickly; they can't believe how fast she was destroyed!*]

11 And the merchants of the earth shall weep and mourn over her [*rather than repenting*]; for no man buyeth their merchandise any more [*because Satan's kingdom has fallen*]:

12 [*In verses 12 and 13, idolatry and accompanying wickedness are described along with materialism.*] The merchandise of gold, and silver, and precious stones, and of pearls, and fine linen, and purple, and silk, and scarlet, and all thyine wood, and all manner vessels of ivory, and all manner vessels of most precious wood, and of brass, and iron, and marble,

13 And cinnamon, and odours [*incense*], and ointments, and frankincense, and wine, and oil, and fine flour, and wheat, and beasts [*domestic animals*], and sheep, and horses, and chariots,

and slaves, and souls of men. [*In other words, everything Satan does has the ultimate goal of trapping the souls of men.*]

14 And the fruits [*the wickedness*] that thy soul lusted [*sinfully chased*] after are departed from thee [*are gone*], and all [*wicked*] things which were dainty and goodly [*which you considered pleasurable*] are departed from thee [*are gone*], and thou shalt find them no more at all [*they are gone permanently*].

You have no doubt noticed that repetition is often used in the scriptures to drive home a point. What you are seeing in John's vision here is an example of this powerful teaching technique used by heaven.

15 The merchants of these things [*wickedness*], which were made rich by her [*Babylon*], shall stand afar off for the fear of her torment, weeping and wailing,

16 And saying, Alas, alas, that great city [*Babylon; in other words, the wickedness of the world sponsored by Satan*], that was clothed in fine linen, and purple, and scarlet, and decked with gold, and precious stones, and pearls!

17 For in one hour [*suddenly*] so great riches is come to nought [*destroyed completely*]. And every shipmaster, and all the company in ships, and sailors, and as many as trade by sea, stood afar off,

Do you get the idea from these many verses that materialism is strongly intertwined with the gross wickedness of the last days?

18 And cried when they saw the smoke of her burning, saying, What city is like unto this great city! [*We thought Babylon (verse 21), Satan's kingdom, was indestructible!*]

19 And they cast dust on their heads [*a sign of extreme mourning in New Testament culture and society*], and cried, weeping and wailing, saying, Alas, alas, that great city, wherein were made rich all that had ships in the sea by reason of her costliness! for in one hour is she made desolate [*our wicked businesses have been destroyed*].

Verse 20, next, tells us that at this point, the inhabitants of heaven will rejoice and the righteous inhabitants of the earth will finally be able to rejoice and be free from the all-pervasive gross wickedness that will permeate societies on earth during the final plagues.

20 Rejoice over her, thou heaven, and ye holy apostles and prophets; for God hath avenged you on her. [*All you righteous who have asked how long it will be before the wicked get what's coming to them (Habakkuk 1:4, D&C 121:2, Revelation 6:10) can now rejoice that the Savior has finally come.*]

21 And a mighty angel took up a stone like a great millstone [*a stone used to grind wheat, commonly used to represent the fate of the wicked; Matthew 18:6*], and cast it into the sea, saying, Thus with violence shall that great city Babylon [*symbolic of Satan's kingdom and his followers*] be thrown down, and shall be found no more at all.

Notice again the use of repetition, in this case to drive home the point that Satan's kingdom of gross wickedness will be completely removed from the earth in preparation for the millennial reign of the Savior.

22 And the voice of harpers, and musicians, and of pipers, and trumpeters, shall be heard no more at all in thee [*Babylon*]; and no craftsman, of whatsoever craft he be, shall be found any more in thee; and the sound of a millstone shall be heard no more

at all in thee [*again, the destruction of Satan's kingdom will be absolute*];

23 And the light of a candle shall shine no more at all in thee; and the voice of the bridegroom and of the bride shall be heard no more at all in thee [*absolute destruction*]: for [*because*] thy [*Babylon's*] merchants were the great men of the earth; for by thy sorceries [*Satan's deceptions*] were all nations deceived.

24 And in her [*Babylon*] was found the blood of prophets, and of saints, and of all that were slain upon the earth [*Babylon is guilty as charged*].

REVELATION 19

After witnessing the destruction of Babylon, as shown in chapter 18, John now sees the faithful Saints praising God for His righteous judgment upon the wicked, which has prepared the way for the Millennium to begin (verses 1–6). The righteous are invited to the marriage supper of the Lamb (verses 7–9), symbolic, in this context, of being invited to join the Savior for the Millennium. John sees the glory, power, and authority of the Savior symbolically coming on a white horse (verse 11) to reign as "KING OF KINGS, AND LORD OF LORDS" (verse 16).

Perhaps you have noticed already that things in Revelation are often not given in chronological order. Such is also the case in this chapter. For example, you will see the arrival of the Millennium, but later, in verse 19, you will read about the final wars and battles on the earth before the Millennium.

1 And after these things [*after the destruction of Satan and his kingdom, Babylon, spoken of in Revelation 18*] I [*John*] heard a great voice of much people in heaven, saying, Alleluia [*"Praise ye the Lord," see Bible Dictionary under "Alleluia"*]; Salvation, and glory, and honour, and power, unto the Lord our God [*the righteous rejoice*]:

2 For true [*exactly on the mark*] and righteous are his judgments: for he hath judged the great whore [*Satan's kingdom; Revelation 17:1, D&C 29:21, 1 Nephi 14:10*], which did corrupt the earth with her fornication [*total disloyalty to God, wickedness, breaking covenants*], and hath avenged the blood of his servants at her hand [*has

punished the wicked for killing the Saints; Revelation 18:20*].

JST Revelation 19:2

2 For true and righteous are his judgments; for he hath judged the great whore, which did corrupt the earth with her fornication, and hath avenged the blood of his saints at her hand.

3 And again they said, Alleluia. And her smoke rose up for ever and ever [*Babylon's destruction is complete; Revelation 18:18*].

Remember that, at this point, Babylon or Satan's kingdom will be destroyed from the earth for the thousand years of the Millennium. Then, at the end of the Millennium, Satan and his evil hosts will be "loosed for a little season" (D&C 88:111), at which time he will gather all of his forces for the final battle, often called the Battle of Gog and Magog (see Bible Dictionary under "Gog"). This battle is described in D&C 88:112–15. This will be the conclusion of the war in heaven that started in our premortal existence (Revelation 12:7–9) when Satan rebelled and drew "a third part of the hosts of heaven" (D&C 29:36; Revelation 12:4). The result of this final battle will be that Satan and his followers will be cast out permanently such that "they shall not have power over the saints any more at all" (D&C 88:114).

Next, John sees many of the characters he has seen during the vision at this point finally rejoicing in the triumph of righteousness.

4 And the four and twenty elders [*the twenty-four faithful Elders from John's day, who had died; Revelation 4:4, D&C 77:5*] and the four beasts [*Revelation 4:6, defined in D&C 77:2–4*] fell down and worshipped God that sat on the throne, saying, Amen; Alleluia.

5 And a voice came out of the throne, saying, Praise our God, all ye his servants [*the righteous*], and ye that fear [*respect*] him, both small and great.

JST Revelation 19:5

5 And a voice came out of the throne, saying, Praise our God, all ye his saints, and ye that fear him, both small and great.

6 And I heard as it were the voice of a great multitude, and as the voice of many waters, and as the voice of mighty thunderings, saying, Alleluia: for the Lord God omnipotent reigneth. [*Finally, the Millennium is here and Jesus is our King!*]

7 Let us be glad and rejoice, and give honour to him: for the marriage of the Lamb is come [*the Savior has come to join with the righteous for a thousand years*], and his wife [*the Church, the righteous Saints*] hath made herself ready [*they are prepared for him; they have oil in their lamps; see Matthew 25:4*].

8 And to her [*the Church, the righteous*] was granted that she should be arrayed in fine linen, clean and white [*dressed in white robes, symbolic of exaltation*]: for the fine linen is the righteousness of saints [*they are clothed with personal righteousness; the Savior's Atonement can do this for us, after all we can do; 2 Nephi 9:14; 25:23*].

Next, in verses 9–10, we see a tender scene in which the angel who has presented this vision to John (Revelation 1:1) instructs him to write a summary statement in his record that emphasizes again the happy state of the righteous. The angel bears his testimony to John.

Then, we see John the Beloved humbly and reverently bow down to worship the angel, perhaps with emotions similar to those in the hearts of the Nephite disciples who began to pray to Jesus (3 Nephi 19:18–22). The angel quickly stops John and humbly assures him that he is merely a fellow servant with John in the service of the Lord. It will be interesting someday to find out who this angel is.

9 And he [*the angel in Revelation 1:1*] saith unto me [*John*], Write, Blessed are they which are called unto the marriage supper of the Lamb [*the righteous who are called up to meet and be with the Savior at his coming; D&C 88:96*]. And he saith unto me, These are the true sayings of God [*the angel bears his testimony to John*].

10 And I [*John*] fell at his [*the angel's*] feet to worship him. And he said unto me, See thou do it not: I am thy fellowservant, and of thy brethren that have the testimony of Jesus: worship God [*don't worship me, worship God; I am one of you, one of the prophets (Revelation 22:9)*]: for the testimony of Jesus is the spirit of prophecy.

JST Revelation 19:10

10 And I fell at his feet to worship him. And he said unto me, See that thou do it not; I am thy fellow servant, and of thy brethren that have the testimony of Jesus; worship God; for the

testimony of Jesus is the spirit of prophecy.

Did you notice the definition of the "spirit of prophecy" in verse 10, above? It is "the testimony of Jesus." One application of this doctrine is that in order to know that Jesus is the Christ, it has to be revealed to us by the Holy Ghost (1 Corinthians 12:3). In that sense, we have the spirit of prophecy in us and can testify to others that Christ will indeed come as the scriptures teach.

11 And I saw heaven opened, and behold a white horse [*symbolic of the triumph of righteousness*]; and he [*Christ*] that sat upon him was called Faithful and True, and in righteousness he doth judge [*the Father turns all judgment over to the Son; John 5:22*] and make war [*destroy the wicked with Satan's kingdom*].

JST Revelation 19:11

11 And I saw heaven opened, and behold a white horse; and he that sat upon him is called Faithful and True, and in righteousness he doth judge and make war;

Did you notice that the words "Faithful" and "True" are capitalized in verse 11, above? Capitalizing these words is the way the printers of the Bible indicate to the reader that these words refer to the Savior and are among the many names of the Savior in the scriptures.

12 His [*Christ's*] eyes were as a flame of fire, and on his head were many crowns [*Christ rules over many kingdoms; D&C 88:50–61*]; and he had a name written [*new name, Revelation 2:17; symbolic of celestial glory; D&C 130:11*], that no man knew, but he himself.

JST Revelation 19:12

12 His eyes as a flame of fire; and he had on his head many crowns; and a name written, that no man knew, but himself.

13 And he was clothed with a vesture dipped in blood [*He wore red at his coming, D&C 133:48, symbolic of the blood of the wicked as judgment falls upon them, D&C 133:50–51*]: and his name is called The Word of God [*another name for Christ; John 1:1*].

JST Revelation 19:13

13 And he is clothed with a vesture dipped in blood; and his name is called The Word of God.

14 And the armies which were in heaven [*the hosts of heaven*]

followed him upon white horses [*symbolic of righteous victory*], clothed in fine linen [*personal righteousness and worthiness; Revelation 19:8*], white and clean.

The JST makes significant changes to verse 15, next.

15 And out of his mouth goeth a sharp sword, that with it he should smite the nations: and he shall rule them with a rod of iron [*the word of God; 1 Nephi 11:25*]: and he treadeth the winepress of the fierceness and wrath of Almighty God. [*He destroys the wicked.*]

JST Revelation 19:15

15 And out of his mouth proceedeth the word of God, and with it he will smite the nations; and he will rule them with the word of his mouth; and he treadeth the winepress in the fierceness and wrath of Almighty God.

With just a few symbolic words, verse 16, next, reviews the destruction of the wicked at the Second Coming.

16 And he hath on his vesture [*robe: Strong's, #2440*] and on his thigh [*hip: German Bible. Symbolic of great slaughter at Christ's coming. See Judges 15:8 where a*]

terrible slaughter is described as "smote them hip and thigh with a great slaughter."] a name written, KING OF KINGS, AND LORD OF LORDS [*in other words, He is Jesus Christ!*].

JST Revelation 19:16

16 And he hath on a vesture, and on his thigh a name written, KING OF KINGS, AND LORD OF LORDS.

17 And I saw an angel standing in the sun [*symbolic of power and authority in heaven*]; and he cried with a loud voice, saying to all the fowls that fly in the midst of heaven, Come and gather yourselves together unto the supper of the great God [*symbolically, many carrion birds are needed to clean up the carcasses of the wicked who will be destroyed in the final wars before the Second Coming*];

18 That ye may eat the flesh of kings [*wicked, influential leaders*], and the flesh of captains, and the flesh of mighty men, and the flesh of horses [*horses are symbolic of military might, weapons of war, and destruction*], and of them that sit on them, and the flesh of all men, both free and bond, both small and great [*all the wicked; none who deserve them*

will escape the judgments and punishments of God].

JST Revelation 19:18

18 That ye may eat the flesh of kings, and the flesh of captains, and the flesh of mighty men, and the flesh of horses, and of them that sit on them, and the flesh of all who fight against the Lamb, both bond and free, both small and great.

19 And I saw the beast [*perhaps referring back to Revelation 13:1*], and the [*wicked*] kings of the earth, and their armies, gathered together to make war against him [*Christ, verse 11*] that sat on the horse, and against his army [*the final battles*].

20 And the beast was taken [*conquered*], and with him the false prophet that wrought miracles before him [*Revelation 13:14*], with which he deceived them that had received the mark of the beast [*Revelation 13:16*], and them that worshipped his image [*his followers; Revelation 13:14*]. These both were cast alive into a lake of fire burning with brimstone [*in other words, you can't imagine how miserable it will be for the wicked; compare with D&C 19:15*].

21 And the remnant [*those wicked who survive the horrible final*

battles before the Second Coming] were slain with the sword of him that sat upon the horse, [*verse 11, above; in other words, they were destroyed at the Second Coming*] which sword proceeded out of his mouth: and all the fowls [*the carrion birds in verse 17*] were filled with their flesh [*the carcasses of the slain wicked in verse 18*].

JST Revelation 19:21

21 And the remnant were slain with the word of him that sat upon the horse, which word proceeded out of his mouth; and all the fowls were filled with their flesh.

REVELATION 20

This chapter is packed with doctrinal details. In it, we see the binding of Satan for the duration of the Millennium (verses 1–2). We see the righteous, resurrected Saints reigning with Christ a thousand years (verse 4). Then we see Satan "loosed a little season" (verse 7) at the end of the Millennium, which leads to the battle of Gog and Magog (verse 8). At the end of this battle, we see the total defeat of the devil and the hosts of the wicked (verses 9–10). Finally, we see the last resurrection and final judgment (verses 12–15).

1 And I saw an angel come down from heaven, having the key of the bottomless pit and a great chain in his hand [*fully equipped to bind Satan*].

JST Revelation 20:1

1 And I saw an angel come down out of heaven, having the key of the bottomless pit and a great chain in his hand.

2 And he laid hold on the dragon, that old serpent, which is the Devil, and Satan, and bound him a thousand years [*during the Millennium*],

From verse 2, above, we see that Satan is bound for the duration of the Millennium and is not even allowed to try to tempt the people living on the earth during the thousand years. This doctrine is taught clearly in D&C 101:28.

D&C 101:28

28 And in that day [*the Millennium*] Satan shall not have power to tempt any man.

Occasionally, someone refers to 1 Nephi 22:26, suggesting that it will only be "because of the righteousness of his people" that "Satan has no power" during the Millennium. In other words, he will still be here, tempting and attempting to lead people astray, but none will follow him. Apostle (later a president of the Church) Joseph Fielding Smith addressed this issue as follows:

"There are many among us who teach that the binding of Satan will be merely the binding which those dwelling on the earth will place upon him by their refusal to hear his enticings. This is not so. He will not have the privilege during that period of time to tempt any man (D&C 101:28)" (Smith, *Church History and Modern Revelation*, 1:192).

3 And cast him into the bottomless pit [*the depths of hell*], and shut him up, and set a seal upon him, that he should deceive the nations no more, till the thousand years should be fulfilled [*are over*]: and after that he must be loosed a little season [*D&C 88:110–15*].

4 And I saw thrones [*symbolic of being joint heirs with Christ; Romans 8:17; in other words, exaltation*], and they [*the righteous*] sat upon them, and judgment was given unto them [*to help rule and reign with the Savior during the Millennium—see end of this verse*]: and I saw the souls [*resurrected bodies*] of them that were beheaded for the witness of

Jesus [*righteous martyrs*], and for the word of God, and which had not worshipped the beast [*Revelation 13; in other words, the righteous who had not followed Satan*], neither his image [*Revelation 13:14*], neither had received his mark upon their foreheads, or in their hands [*Revelation 13:16*]; and they [*the righteous*] lived and reigned with Christ a thousand years.

5 But the rest of the dead [*the wicked*] lived not again [*were not resurrected*] until the thousand years were finished [*D&C 88:100–102*]. This [*the resurrection of the righteous indicated in verse 4; see D&C 88:97–98*] is the first resurrection [*which takes place at the beginning of the Millennium*].

6 Blessed and holy is he that hath part in the first resurrection: on such the second death [*spiritual death; being cut off from God's presence; Alma 12:16–18, 32*] hath no power, but they shall be priests of God and of Christ, and shall reign with him a thousand years.

JST Revelation 20:6

6 Blessed and holy are they who have part in the first resurrection; on such the second death hath no power, but they

shall be priests of God and of Christ, and shall reign with him a thousand years.

Verse 7, next, sets the stage for the final battle between good and evil on this earth. It is usually called the Battle of Gog and Magog (verse 8). By the way, Gog was an ancient wicked king over the wicked kingdom of Magog (see note in verse 8, below). He and his evil empire have since become symbolic of the devil and his kingdom.

7 And when the thousand years are expired, Satan shall be loosed out of his prison [*D&C 88:111*],

8 And shall go out to deceive the nations which are in the four quarters of the earth, Gog and Magog [*symbolic of wicked nations and their leaders; for a definition of Gog, see Bible Dictionary under "Gog," and for Magog, under "Magog"*], to gather them together to battle: the number of whom is as the sand of the sea [*there will be great numbers of wicked during the little season after the end of the Millennium*].

9 And they [*the wicked; Gog and Magog*] went up on the breadth of the earth, and compassed the camp of the saints about [*made*

war against the Saints; *D&C 88:112–15*], and the beloved city [*the Lord's kingdom*]: and fire came down from God out of heaven, and devoured them.

Among the doctrines we might glean from verse 9, above, is the comforting eternal truth that God has absolute power to defeat the devil and the wicked who follow him.

10 And the devil that deceived them was cast into the lake of fire and brimstone, where the beast [*Revelation 13*] and the false prophet are, and shall be tormented day and night for ever and ever. [*Satan and his wicked hosts are cast out forever—see D&C 76:32–36, 44–45; 88:111–15.*]

11 And I saw a great white throne, and him [*Christ; Revelation 21:5–6*] that sat on it, from whose face the earth and the heaven fled away; and there was found no place for them. [*In other words, there will be a new heaven and new earth (not a different earth, but a resurrected one; D&C 88:26, 130:9) after the Millennium and little season are over and the earth is celestialized (D&C 130:9–11), perhaps referring to a different set of stars and constellations in our sky because "this earth will be rolled back into the presence of God, and crowned*

with celestial glory" (Smith, TPJS, p. 181).]

Next in the vision, John is shown the last judgment. He has already seen the righteous resurrected, judged, and empowered to rule and reign with Christ during the Millennium, in verse 4, above. Therefore, it is likely that verse 12, next, refers to the wicked who were not resurrected until the end of the Millennium (verse 5, above). If this is the case, it is the wicked who now stand before the Savior (John 5:22) to be judged.

However, it is also possible that verses 12–13, next, are a brief review and summary of the final judgment of all. Either way, John has been shown the judgment of the righteous and the wicked in this segment of the vision.

12 And I saw the dead, small and great [*in other words, from all walks of life*], stand before God; and the books were opened: and another book was opened, which is the book of life [*a book kept in heaven which contains the names and deeds of the righteous—see Bible Dictionary under "Book of Life"*]: and the dead were judged out of those things which were written in the books, according to their works.

13 And the sea gave up the dead which were in it; and death and hell delivered up the dead which were in them [*all the wicked were finally resurrected also; D&C 88:101–2*]: and they were judged every man according to their works.

14 And death and hell were cast into the lake of fire. This is the second death [*being cut off completely from God and any kingdom of glory; only sons of perdition will suffer this forever; D&C 76:36–37*].

15 And whosoever was not found written in the book of life was cast into the lake of fire. [*All except sons of perdition are saved at least to some degree, by Christ, into the telestial, terrestrial, or celestial kingdoms; see D&C 76:37–39, 81–87.*]

REVELATION 21

In this chapter, John describes the earth as it attains celestial glory. It is a pleasant reminder that the rewards and blessings that our Father in Heaven has in store for the righteous are far beyond our capability to imagine. In other words, one of the messages of John the Beloved to us is that it is worth striving to be faithful to the gospel of Jesus Christ no matter what the cost.

1 And I saw a new heaven and a new earth [*D&C 29:23–24; see also notes for Revelation 20:11 in this study guide*]: for the first heaven and the first earth were passed away; and there was no more sea.

2 And I John saw the holy city, new Jerusalem, coming down from God out of heaven, prepared as a bride adorned for her husband [*dressed in her finest; in other words, dressed in personal righteousness and covenant keeping, worthy to join Christ in celestial glory*].

3 And I heard a great voice out of heaven saying, Behold, the tabernacle [*physical body*] of God is with men [*the Savior is literally, physically, here with us*], and he will dwell with them, and they shall be his people, and God himself shall be with them, and be their God. [*Christ will dwell with the righteous on the celestialized earth; see D&C 130:9.*]

Referring to verses 2 and 3, above, we see that, according to Ether 13:8–10, a city called "New Jerusalem" will be built

upon the American continent (see also the tenth article of faith). Moses 7:22 tells us that this New Jerusalem will be built up by the righteous as they look forward to the coming of Christ. In his vision, John saw "the holy city, new Jerusalem, coming down from God out of heaven" (verse 3). We understand the "new Jerusalem" that John saw here to be a different city than the New Jerusalem described in Ether and Moses. The "new Jerusalem" seen by John seems to be symbolic of this earth as it is celestialized and as it becomes the abode of the Savior and the righteous Saints forever (see verse 3). Bruce R. McConkie said: "When this earth becomes a celestial sphere 'that great city, the holy Jerusalem,' shall again descend 'out of heaven from God,' as this earth becomes the abode of celestial beings forever (Revelation 21:10–27)" (McConkie, *DNTC*, 3:580–81).

In verse 4, next, we see a most beautiful reminder that it is worth whatever it takes to become worthy of celestial glory.

4 And God shall wipe away all tears from their eyes; and there

shall be no more death, neither sorrow, nor crying, neither shall there be any more pain [*a beautiful description of celestial glory*]: for the former things [*past troubles, including struggles during mortality to remain worthy*] are passed away.

5 And he [*Christ; Revelation 20:11, 21:6*] that sat upon the throne said, Behold, I make all things new. And he said unto me, Write: for these words are true and faithful [*Christ bears testimony to John of the truthfulness of the things he is seeing and hearing*].

6 And he [*Christ*] said unto me [*John*], It is done [*everything is fulfilled; D&C 1:38*]. I am Alpha and Omega, the beginning and the end. I will give unto him [*the righteous*] that is athirst of the fountain of the water of life freely [*living water; John 4:14*].

7 He that overcometh [*overcomes sin and wickedness*] shall inherit all things [*will receive exaltation, D&C 132:20*]; and I will be his God, and he shall be my son [*Mosiah 5:7*].

8 But the fearful [*perhaps meaning those who are afraid to do right*], and unbelieving, and the abominable, and murderers, and whoremongers, and sorcerers, and idolaters, and all liars, shall have their part [*will receive their punishment*] in the lake which burneth with fire and brimstone: which is the second death.

9 And there came unto me one of the seven angels [*Revelation 15:1*] which had the seven vials full of the seven last plagues, and talked with me, saying, Come hither, I will shew thee the bride, the Lamb's wife. [*There are many possible meanings for this, including the Church, the righteous, the City of Enoch, the celestial city or kingdom described in verses 11–27 of this chapter.*]

10 And he carried me away in the spirit to a great and high mountain, and shewed me that great city, the holy Jerusalem [*in this context symbolic of the celestial kingdom*], descending out of heaven from God,

In other words, John is shown the beauty and glory of the celestial kingdom.

11 Having the glory of God: and her light [*the city's light*] was like unto a stone most precious, even like a jasper stone, clear as crystal;

12 And had a wall great and high

[*symbolic of security, safety*], and had twelve [*symbolic of divine government—see symbolism notes at the beginning of this study guide*] gates, and at the gates twelve angels, and names written thereon, which are the names of the twelve tribes of the children of Israel:

13 On the east three gates; on the north three gates; on the south three gates; and on the west three gates. [*Perhaps the use of sets of "three" symbolizes that the whole celestial city or kingdom is blessed with the presence of the Godhead—see symbolism notes referred to above.*]

14 And the wall of the city had twelve foundations, and in them the names of the twelve apostles of the Lamb [*perhaps symbolizing that the city is indeed built upon the righteous principles and priesthood covenants taught by the twelve Apostles*].

15 And he that talked with me had a golden reed [*perhaps a celestial measuring device similar to the reed in Revelation 11:1, used here to show John that things indeed "measure up" just as promised*] to measure the city, and the gates thereof, and the wall thereof.

16 And the city lieth foursquare, and the length is as large as the breadth: and he measured the city with the reed, twelve thousand furlongs [*if a furlong is about 220 yards, Bible Dictionary under "Weights and Measures," and the length and breadth are twelve thousand furlongs each, the city that John saw was about 1,500 U.S. miles in length, width, and height, or about 3 billion, 375 million cubic miles of living space, perhaps symbolizing to John that there is plenty of glorious living space for the "great multitude" of the righteous that he saw in heaven in Revelation 7:9; see also D&C 76:67*]. The length and the breadth and the height of it are equal.

Verse 16, above, is very encouraging because, as mentioned in the note within the verse, it reminds us that, because of the effectiveness of the Father's plan, a great many of His children will ultimately choose to accept the gospel and return home to Him. Among other things, this implies that there will be a great deal of success in the preaching of the gospel in the post-mortal spirit world. A quote from President Wilford Woodruff is helpful in this regard. Speaking of the redemption of the dead and temple work we do for our ancestors, he quoted D&C 137:7–9 and then said:

"So it will be with your fathers [ancestors]. There will be very few, if any, who will not accept the Gospel. . . . The fathers of this people will embrace the Gospel" (Woodruff, *Teachings of Presidents of the Church*, pp. 190–91).

17 And he [*the angel talking to John in verse 15*] measured the wall thereof, an hundred and forty and four cubits, according to the measure of a man, that is, of the angel.

JST Revelation 21:17

17 And he measured the wall thereof, a hundred and forty and four cubits, according to the measure of a man, that is, of the angel.

John now attempts the impossible; in other words, to describe to us the beauty of the dwellings for the righteous on this celestialized earth and celestial glory. He will employ the highest descriptive superlatives, using beautiful and precious jewel stones and such from his day and culture.

18 And the building of the wall of it was of jasper: and the city was pure gold, like unto clear glass.

19 And the foundations of the wall of the city were garnished [*beautified, made pleasant to look at*] with all manner of precious stones. The first foundation was jasper; the second, sapphire; the third, a chalcedony [*a kind of light green quartz*]; the fourth, an emerald;

20 The fifth, sardonyx; the sixth, sardius; the seventh, chrysolite; the eighth, beryl; the ninth, a topaz; the tenth, a chrysoprasus; the eleventh, a jacinth; the twelfth, an amethyst.

21 And the twelve gates were twelve pearls; every several gate was of one pearl: and the street of the city was pure gold, as it were transparent glass.

Next, we are taught that the whole of the celestial kingdom is a temple, having the presence of the Father and the Son on it.

22 And I saw no temple therein [*a temple is not needed*]: for the Lord God Almighty and the Lamb are the temple of it.

23 And the city had no need of the sun, neither of the moon, to shine in it: for the glory of God did lighten it, and the Lamb [*Christ*] is the light thereof.

24 And the nations of them which are saved [*the righteous*] shall

walk in the light of it: and the kings of the earth [*those of the righteous in celestial glory who are exalted and have thus become "kings and priests unto God" (Revelation 1:6; D&C 76:56–59]* do bring their glory and honour into it.

25 And the gates of it shall not be shut at all by day: for there shall be no night there.

26 And they [*the exalted, mentioned in verse 24, above, who have become gods]* shall bring the glory and honour of the nations into it.

27 And there shall in no wise enter into it any thing that defileth, neither whatsoever worketh abomination, or maketh a lie [*a reiteration of the doctrine that no unclean thing can enter the kingdom; example: 3 Nephi 27:19]*: but they which are written in the Lamb's book of life [*Revelation 20:12; the righteous who have been made clean through the Atonement of Christ; see also Alma 34:36]*.

REVELATION 22

John's vision draws to a close with symbolism and doctrines that summarize major messages

of the book of Revelation, including the fact that the reward of the righteous is wonderful beyond our ability to comprehend and that the wicked are left out of these priceless blessings.

As we start verse 1, we see that it is a continuation of the description of celestial glory from chapter 21.

1 And he [*one of the seven angels; Revelation 21:9]* shewed me a pure river of water of life, clear as crystal, proceeding out of the throne of God and of the Lamb.

2 In the midst of the street of it [*the celestial city, described in chapter 21; in other words, celestial glory]*, and on either side of the river, was there the tree of life [*1 Nephi 8:10; Revelation 22:14]*, which bare twelve manner of fruits, and yielded her fruit every month [*the benefits of the gospel are not seasonal, rather continue constantly forever]*: and the leaves of the tree were for the healing of the nations [*what the gospel can do for people]*.

3 And there shall be no more curse [*on the earth, as described in Genesis 3:17–18, which will then be the celestial kingdom, D&C 130:9; 88:25]*: but the throne of God and of the Lamb shall be

in it; and his servants shall serve him:

4 And they shall see his face; and his name shall be in their foreheads [*Revelation 3:12; meaning that they have taken His name upon them and kept their covenants, therefore they will be with Him in celestial glory*].

5 And there shall be no night there; and they need no candle, neither light of the sun; for the Lord God giveth them light: and they shall reign for ever and ever [*they will be Gods; D&C 132:20*].

6 And he said unto me, These sayings are faithful and true [*the angel bears his testimony to John*]: and the Lord God of the holy prophets sent his angel to shew unto his servants the things which must shortly be done [*the vision is now coming to a close and the angel is summarizing for John*].

Next, the angel speaks directly for the Savior in what was explained in the notes associated with JST, Revelation 1:1, in this study guide, as "divine investiture."

7 Behold, I [*Christ*] come quickly [*not "soon," but when the time is right, He will come suddenly upon the wicked as a thief in the night;*

D&C 106:4–5]: blessed is he that keepeth [*obeys*] the sayings of the prophecy of this book.

In verses 8–9, next, John reviews something he already recorded for us in Revelation 19:10. It may be that this experience made such an impression on him that he wanted to use it as a personal object lesson to remind us not to worship anyone or anything other than God. As we follow this counsel, it will give us additional strength to avoid the pitfalls Satan has created for us in the last days.

8 And I John saw these things, and heard them. And when I had heard and seen, I fell down to worship before the feet of the angel which shewed me these things.

9 Then saith he unto me, See thou do it not [*don't worship me*]: for I am thy fellowservant, and of thy brethren the prophets [*I am one of you*], and of them which keep the sayings of this book: worship God.

JST Revelation 22:9

9 Then saith he unto me, See that thou do it not; for I am thy fellowservant, and of thy brethren the prophets, and of them

which keep the sayings of this book; worship God.

10 And he saith unto me, Seal not the sayings of the prophecy of this book [*let these things be read*]: for the time is at hand.

The last phrase of verse 10, above, appears to be a repetition of the same phrase found in chapter 1, verse 3. The JST of this phrase in JST, Revelation 1:3 is given as, "for the time of the coming of the Lord draweth nigh." Thus, "the time is at hand," repeated twice, seems to serve as "bookends" for the Revelation of John. It may be considered to be a strong statement to us who live in the last days, that when we see the things taking place spoken of in the vision given to John, we can be assured that the coming of the Lord is indeed getting close.

Next, in verse 11, we see that the time will eventually come for all of us when the opportunity for preparing for judgment day will be over.

11 He that is unjust, let him be unjust still: and he which is filthy, let him be filthy still: and he that is righteous, let him be righteous still: and he that is holy, let him be holy still [*when final judgment*

comes, you will be judged according to what you are].

12 And, behold, I [*Christ*] come quickly; and my reward is with me, to give every man according as his work shall be.

13 I am Alpha and Omega [*Revelation 1:11*], the beginning and the end, the first and the last [*in other words, Christ is the "A" and the "Z"; He knows the beginning from the end; He was there at the beginning of creation and He will be there at the end of the earth to judge us; He is in charge of all things under the direction of the Father*].

14 Blessed are they that do his commandments, that they may have right to the tree of life [*spoken of in verse 2*], and may enter in through the gates into the city [*the celestial kingdom*].

Verse 15, next, gives us a brief description of those who will receive telestial glory. (Compare with D&C 76:103.)

15 For without [*meaning outside of the celestial kingdom, spoken of in verse 14, above, specifically telestial glory*] are dogs [*an unclean beast under the law of Moses (Leviticus 11:27), perhaps symbolic here of people who refused to make themselves*

clean through the Atonement], and sorcerers, and whoremongers [*people who constantly seek opportunities for immorality*], and murderers, and idolaters, and whosoever loveth and maketh a lie [*people who are dishonest, love to lie*].

Just an additional note about "dogs" in verse 15, above. This term was often used in New Testament times to refer to Gentiles who were not members of the Church and who lived lifestyles contrary to the gospel. See footnote 27a for Mark 7:27 in the LDS version of the English Bible.

Next, the Savior bears His testimony to John that He is the Redeemer, about whom the Old Testament prophesied.

16 I Jesus have sent mine angel to testify unto you these things in the churches [*probably meaning the seven churches or "wards" referred to in Revelation 1:11*]. I am the root [*that came out of dry ground; apostate Judaism, as stated by Isaiah in Isaiah 53:2*] and the offspring of David [*a descendent of David*], and the bright and morning star [*the first and the brightest; in other words, I am the Savior*].

17 And the Spirit [*the Holy Ghost*] and the bride [*the righteous members of the Church; see Revelation 21:2*] say, Come. And let him that heareth say, Come. And let him that is athirst come. And whoso ever will, let him take the water of life freely [*an open invitation to all to come unto Christ*].

Perhaps you have run into the argument by other Christians that our Book of Mormon and other scriptures in addition to the Bible violate Revelation 22:18. They suggest that nothing should be added to the Bible. Pay close attention to the notes in verses 18–19, next, for the solution to this challenge.

18 For I testify unto every man that heareth the words of the prophecy of this book [*the book of Revelation, not the whole Bible*], If any man shall add unto these things [*intentionally twists meanings or adds false doctrines*], God shall add unto him the plagues that are written in this book:

19 And if any man shall take away from the words of the book of this prophecy, God shall take away his part out of the book of life, and out of the holy city [*celestial glory—see Revelation 21:10*], and from the things which are written in this book [*don't*]

intentionally twist the meanings, delete doctrines, etc., from the book of Revelation].

The same basic message and warning found in verses 18–19, above, are found in the Bible in Deuteronomy.

Deuteronomy 4:2

2 Ye shall not add unto the word which I command you, neither shall ye diminish *ought* from it, that ye may keep the commandments of the LORD your God which I command you.

So, you can see that if someone who believes only in the Bible wants to challenge the Church for having additional scripture by referring to Revelation 22:18–19, one can readily refer to Deuteronomy 4:2, and, using the same false logic, suggest that nothing should be in the Bible that was written after Deuteronomy 4:2.

20 He which testifieth these things saith, Surely I come quickly. Amen. Even so, come, Lord Jesus [*John's final fervent plea, here*].

Next, in verse 21, John addresses his readers, including you and me, with a tender blessing upon us. All of Paul's epistles have such a statement or blessing upon his readers at or near the end of the last chapter.

21 The grace of our Lord Jesus Christ be with you all. Amen.

SOURCES

Gospel Principles. Salt Lake City: The Church of Jesus Christ of Latter-day Saints, 2009.

Holland, Jeffrey R. *Christ and the New Covenant: The Messianic Message of the Book of Mormon.* Salt Lake City: Deseret Book, 1997.

Holland, Jeffery R. "This Do in Remembrance of Me." *Ensign*, Nov. 1995, 65.

McConkie, Bruce R. *Doctrinal New Testament Commentary* (*DNTC*). 3 vols. Salt Lake City: Bookcraft, 1965–73.

McConkie, Bruce R. *Mormon Doctrine.* 2nd ed. Salt Lake City: Bookcraft, 1966.

Millet, Robert L. *Alive in Christ: The Miracle of Spiritual Rebirth.* Salt Lake City: Deseret Book, 1997.

Nelson, Russell M. "Divine Love." *Ensign*, Feb. 2003, 20–25.

Parry, Jay and Parry, Donald. *Understanding the Book of Revelation.* Salt Lake City: Deseret Book, 2007.

Perry, L. Tom. "If Ye Are Prepared Ye Shall Not Fear." *Ensign*, Nov. 1995, p. 36.

Pratt, Orson. *Journal of Discourses.* 26 vols. London: Latter-day Saints' Book Depot, 1854–86.

Smith, Joseph. *History of The Church of Jesus Christ of Latter-day Saints (HC).* Edited by B. H. Roberts. 2d. ed. rev., 7 vols. Salt Lake City: The Church of Jesus Christ of Latter-day Saints, 1932–51.

Smith, Joseph. *Teachings of the Prophet Joseph Smith* (*TPJS*). Selected by Joseph Fielding Smith. Salt Lake City: Deseret Book, 1976.

Smith, Joseph Fielding. *Church History and Modern Revelation.* 4 vols. Salt Lake City: the Council of the Twelve Apostles, 1947.

Smith, Joseph Fielding. *Doctrines of Salvation.* Compiled by Bruce R. McConkie. 3 vols. Salt Lake City: Bookcraft, 1954–56.

Strong, James. *The Exhaustive Concordance of the Bible.* Nashville: Abingdon, 1890.

Talmage, James E. *Articles of Faith.* Salt Lake City: The Church of Jesus Christ of Latter-day Saints, 1977.

Teachings of Presidents of the Church, Brigham Young. Salt Lake City: The Church of Jesus Christ of Latter-day Saints, 1997.

Teachings of Presidents of the Church, Wilford Woodruff. Salt Lake City: The Church of Jesus Christ of Latter-day Saints, 2004.

The Life and Teachings of Jesus and His Apostles. Institute of Religion New Testament Student Manual. Salt Lake City: The Church of Jesus Christ of Latter-day Saints, 1978–79.

The Words of Joseph Smith. Religious Studies Center. Provo, Utah: Brigham Young University, 1980.

"The Temple Worker's Excursion." *Young Women's Journal,* Aug. 1894, 512.

ABOUT THE AUTHOR

David J. Ridges taught for the Church Educational System for thirty-five years and has taught for several years at BYU Campus Education Week. He taught adult religion classes and Know Your Religion classes for BYU Continuing Education for many years. He has also served as a curriculum writer for Sunday School, seminary, and institute of religion manuals.

He has served in many callings in the Church, including Gospel Doctrine teacher, bishop, stake president, and patriarch. He and Sister Ridges served a full-time eighteen-month mission, training senior CES missionaries and helping coordinate their assignments throughout the world.

Brother Ridges and his wife, Janette, are the parents of six children and make their home in Springville, Utah.